Larry Barton, PhD

JESUS
THE RENEGADE

This publication contains the opinions and ideas of its author. It is intended to provide helpful and informative material on the subjects addressed in the publication. The author and publisher specifically disclaim all responsibility for any liability, loss or risk, personal or otherwise, which is incurred as a consequence, directly or indirectly, of the use and application of any of the contents of this book.

WORKBOOK PRESS LLC
187 E Warm Springs Rd,
Suite B285, Las Vegas, NV 89119, USA

Website: https://workbookpress.com/
Hotline: 1-888-818-4856
Email: admin@workbookpress.com

Ordering Information:
Quantity sales. Special discounts are available on quantity purchases by corporations, associations, and others. For details, contact the publisher at the address above.

Library of Congress Control Number:
ISBN-13:   978-1-961845-65-7 (Paperback Version)
              978-1-961845-64-0 (Digital Version)

REV. DATE: 06/16/2023

JESUS

THE RENEGADE

Larry Barton, PhD

ACKNOWLEDGEMENTS

Special thanks to my wife Mary Barton for working long hours to help make this possible. I would also like to thank Breanna Goray, Christy Stone, and Amanda McLain for their untitring assistance and long hours type setting, proof reading, and editing. I would also like to thank my life long pastor friend, Larry Wells. He has always been available to keep my antique computer and printers up and running.

For more information about the author, please contact:

Larry Barton

P O Box 588

Talladega, Al 35161

Mayorlarrybarton@aol.com

https://authorlarrybarton.com/

PREFACE

Having been born in 1940, an era where people were either Baptist or Methodist in their religious belief, my parents were considered different due to them being members of The Church of God. One time, in the mid forties, mother was refused a job in a textile plant due to her being a member of an organization, referred to as a "Holy Roller" a Tongue Speaking religious group.

As a small boy from as far back as I can remember, I was taught to believe that God was real and Jesus was his Son. I was taught that when one dies, they would either spend eternity in hell or heaven, depending as to where you had been saved or reborn again. My mom and dad always said the blessing before each meal, thanking God for what we had been given to eat and there was always Bible reading followed by prayers at night, before we went to sleep.

Wednesday and Friday evenings, and twice on Sunday was reserved for church services. However, there was always week long revival services through out the year. The minister always preached hell fire, brimstone and damnation and how it was a sin for women to cut their hair, wear jewelry, wear makeup, shave their legs and they are to only wear clothing designed for women. Pant suits were forbidden as well as going to the movies. The T.V. was a product of the devil, it was referred to as the devil's workshop. He preached that the use of tobacco or alcohol products was a fast tract to hell.

Many of the people in the early 40's and 50's, who were members of the holiness movement had not been educated formally and even though they could read and write, they were taught to depend strictly on the preacher to interpret the word of God and never to doubt anything he preached to them.

The congregation was taught that the Bible was the inspired word of God and that Jesus was born of a virgin. Although the preacher never dwelled on how Mary, the mother of Jesus had gotten pregnant by the Holy Ghost, this was not something that was questioned. To question what the preacher said about the Bible, would be a form of blasphemy.

As I became older, I had a strong desire to learn more about the Bible, I read daily and researched the scriptures. I began to read as many books as I could, trying to learn more about God, Jesus and his life. The more I read, the more questions I had about the Bible and some of it's contents.

Years later I asked mother, who was very dedicated to daily Bible reading and prayer, if the Bible taught that it was a sin to wear jewelry, women to cut their hair, attending movie theatres, watching T.V. and all the other things that we had been taught would send one to hell for doing -- was it all really in the Bible? She said no, that this is the way she had been taught growing up and the doctrine was just passed on from the older generation. Mother lived to be 101 years old and she never changed her belief. However she always told us, if we had to ask if we thought it was wrong to do something, then it was best to not do it.

I do not regret my conservative raising and do not find fault with those who teach and practice this doctrine. I believe in Matthew 7:1-6 and Luke 6:37-42 that each individual shall give an account of himself to God when they pass from this walk of life. Ezekiel 14:1-11 and 1 Corinthians 8:1-13 admonishes us to not judge one another.

While serving 37 months in a prison, I spent many days and hours reading the bible and researching the scriptures. I made notes of various articles written by theologians and Biblical scholars from the past. When i decided to write a book about Jesus, a very diverse individual, I used a lot of the material I had saved along with all my notes and I came up with a book entitled, JESUS THE RENEGADE.

From the time he was conceived in the womb of a virgin, a woman who had never had sex with a man, the story of Jesus continues to create controversy.

How would society react today if an under aged girl living at home, became pregnant and tried to convince her family, boyfriend, folks in the community, and even church members that she had not had sexual intercourse. Probably the same way Joseph acted when Mary shares with him, her husband to be, that she was expecting a baby, but had not had sex with Joseph or any other man.

At first Joseph, being her husband to be, and a righteous man did not want to expose her to public disgrace, so he had in mind to divorce her quietly. However, having considered this, an angel of the Lord appeared to him in a dream and said, "Joseph, son of David, Do not be afraid. Take Mary home as your wife, because what is conceived in her is from the Holy Spirit. She shall give birth to a son and you are to give him the name Jesus, because he will save his people from their sin". (Matthew 1:20).

Having awakened from his dream, he did what the angel of the Lord commanded him to do. Joseph did not have sexual intercourse with Mary until after Jesus was born.

In today's society, what would happen if a single 13 or 14 year old girl, came home one day and shared with her parents that she was pregnant, but did not know how this could've happened because she had never had sexual relations.

According to a recent report, co-authored by an Episcopal Deacon, Several women claim they have became pregnant and have not had intercourse. They claim that they became pregnant the same way that the mother of Jesus did.

Another group claimed that it was a scientific miracle that

caused the pregnancy of Mary. They have the theory that it was Parthenogenesis that caused her pregnancy. Parthenogenesis, is a Greek word meaning it is a natural form of asexual reproduction in which growth and development of embryos occur without fertilization.

After Jesus was born, King Herod, who liked to be referred to as Herod the Great, had a reputation of killing anyone who he felt was a threat to him. He heard about the birth of Jesus through three wise men who had heard about Jesus and was looking for him so they could worship him. Having heard about Jesus, King Herod sent word that he would like to see this Jesus and worship him as well. King Herod did not want to worship Jesus, but wanted to kill him.

God warned the wise men of King Herod's intent and the wise men evaded him. Having realized he had been duped by the wise men, the king issued an order that all children under the age of two were to be killed. Reminds one of what is going on in the far East. However Herod's action was not successful, due to his death shortly after issuing his order.

If a survey was taken of who was the best known controversial person in all the world, without a doubt it would be Jesus. Some may argue that there are some politicians like President Donald Trump and religious leaders, like the Rev T D Jakes and Joel Olsteen, who might run a close race and I agree. However, they cannot touch Jesus in name recognition and controversy.

Politicians become embroiled in controversy by making laws and choosing individuals to serve in their administration. Religious leaders, become tangled up in controversy by trying to run the church and associating with just a few of the influential members. In many cases, the pastor tries to usurp the authority of the deacons. In the case of Jesus, he took on the politicians and religious leaders thus making him a "RENEGADE."

For those who have not read and studied the bible and possibly not involved with church, may not be familiar with this Renegade Jesus. What is it, about Jesus, that makes him so controversial?

From his birth until his death on the cross, Jesus had tongues wagging and religious leaders trying to kill him. He was not part of the establishment and did not mind who's toes he stepped on. He went from town to town teaching and healing the sick, the blind, and raising the dead. He spent time with the sinners accused of having a close relationship with a prostitute and breaking laws of the land. He chose twelve men called disciples, to be with him and travel throughout as he ministered. These twelve Jesus chose, were supposed to be friends, but were similar in character as to those chosen for political positions. Among the twelve was a thief, trader, doubter, fighter, back slider, liar, fanatic, persecutor of church members, skeptic, hypocrite, assassin, high tempered, and one, the treasurer betrayed him. Had Jesus lived today he might have had law suits filed against him for being a Racist;

not choosing a female or minority for a disciple.

As you read Jesus The Renegade, I trust you can see how society is constantly changing and how a lot of things Jesus encountered is still active in society today. They are those who are trying to destroy the word of God by undermining the virgin birth of Jesus. America is less Christian today than it was 20 years ago. Some of this decline has been brought about due to the immorality that exist in many of the mainline churches. According to my life time friend Reverend Max Morris, President of world wide prayer partners, (WWPP), In America they are between 100 to 200 churches closing down weekly. This is an estimate of six to ten thousand churches annually. The comment you hear from many, is why do I want to go to church when the pastor and the members are doing the same things that I'm doing and I don't claim to be a Christian. It was the Christians who wanted Jesus killed.

As a member of society, are you among those who are trying to kill Jesus and destroy the word of God, or will you join Jesus and become one of his Renegades?

The majority of the material in this book is taken from the King James Bible. I have made comments throughout the book comparing Jesus and Politics. I have made effort to give credit to material written by other writers, but also recognizing that some of the writers of their version of what took place during the life of Jesus on Earth could be information passed down by others through the years. It can easily be understood that such accounts from apocryphal and legendary literature may not always be completely accurate. However unless proven false, this material has to be accepted as written. Even some scriptures in the Bible, different writers record events of the day a little different.

While I do not subscribe to all the man made teachings of different denominations and a lot of the material in the Bible is hard for me to swallow, I fully accept that the Bible is the inspired word of God. I am of the opinion, that if the Bible is bogus and a person is just grave yard dead when they die, then they have not lost anything.

However, I am not willing to take a chance that it is not real and face spending eternity in a place called hell. Lastly, I present this material in my book not intending to sway a person and their beliefs, but to present how society has placed their spin on God's Holy Word. I would encourage everyone to research the scriptures, pray and believe that there is a here after and each one will have to give an account over their own actions when death comes calling.

If I have not given proper credit to any author or writer of material included in my book, it is an honest mistake and not intentional.

THE FIRST PUBLIC APPEARANCE OF JESUS

The actual ministry of Jesus did not begin until he was approximately thirty years of age (Luke 3:23 KJV), although he started public speaking much earlier.

At the age of twelve, Joseph and Mary went to Jerusalem after the custom of the feast (Luke 2:42KJV). While there, it is apparent Joseph satisfied the law in paying five shekels ($3.20) in redemption money (Numbers 3:47; 18:16KJV).

Under this law, every Jewish boy becomes "a son of the law"(Luke 2:48-51KJV) at this age. Joseph after having paid the five shekels became afforded the legal right of father; thus claiming the obedience of (Luke 2:48-51KJV) when Mary, the mother of Jesus said unto him, "Son, why hast thou dealt with us? Behold thy father and I have sought the sorrowing."(Luke 2:43-44KJV) Mary was questioning Jesus in reference to him becoming separated from her and Joseph after they had completed their business transaction and set out on their way to return to Nazareth. Mary and Joseph had not been too concerned at first that Jesus was not with them,(Luke 2:43-44KJV) they were of the impression that he was with some of the other friends that had gone to Jerusalem for the feast .

A normal days journey is from eighteen to thirty miles, but it was customary for all caravans to travel from five to ten miles on the first day of their journey for anyone who had been forgotten or left anything behind, they would be able to catch up. Having a days journey (Luke 2:44KJV), estimated to be about eight miles, realizing Jesus was not with the group or caravan, Joseph and Mary returned to Jerusalem seeking him (Luke 2:45KJV). If this event had taken place in modern day, Mary and Joseph could have been charged by the government with child neglect, abandonment or conspiracy. If they had been found guilty, they could have been sentenced to several years in prison.

Three days later however, Joseph and Mary found Jesus, in the temple,(Luke 2:46KJV) sitting in the midst of doctors, listening and asking them questions . All that heard him were astonished at his understanding and answers (Luke 2:47KJV).

Upon finding Jesus, he was questioned about his staying behind (Luke 2:48KJV). Jesus responded by saying, "How is it that ye sought me? Wist ye not that I must be about my fathers' business (Luke 2:49KJV)? This response reflects the first recorded words of Jesus. "It is finished," (John 19:30KJV) was his last recorded words.

Mary and Joseph did not understand the answer Jesus

gave them (Luke2:50KJV), but Mary kept all these saying in her heart (Luke 2:51KJV).

JESUS PREPARES FOR THE MINISTRY

J esus had come from Nazareth of Galilee and requested he be baptized in the river of Jordan by John The Baptist. (Matthew 3:13KJV)

John The Baptist, whose name derives from a Hebrew term, "Jehovah is Gracious", was known as "The Baptist", meaning "an immerser". Jesus referred to him as non greater who was born of a woman (Matthew 11:11KJV). Elizabeth, the mother of John The Baptist, was related to the mother of Jesus (Luke1:36KJV).

The dress code of John The Baptist might have drawn a lot of stares and comments in some churches, but possible would have fit in with some of the street people in today's society. He wore a camel hair garment, secured by a leather belt and his diet was locusts and wild honey (Matthew 3:4KJV). The hair cloak could have been a rough fabric woven from the hair of a camel(Zech 13:4KJV) or made from the skin of a camel. Several of the Old Testament Prophets dressed in this manner

. His dietary meal was what the poorer elements of society ate. Some accused him of having a demon (Matthew 11:18KJV). Eating and drinking stood for socializing and since John was not a party goer,(Mark 5:2-3KJV) many said he was possessed of evil spirits.

John The Baptist was very influential because of his teaching and preaching and known for possible thousands being converted and baptized. His administering baptism was "for the forgiveness of sins"(Mark 1:4KJV). In view of this, John was hesitant in baptizing Jesus (Matthew 3:14KJV). Jesus was sinless (1 Peter 1:19KJV).

Having been baptized, not sprinkled, coming straightway up out of the water, Jesus saw the heavens opened and the Spirit like a dove descended upon him. There came a voice from heaven saying, "Thou art my beloved Son in whom I am well pleased." (Matthew 4:16-17KJV).Jesus was immediately driven into the wilderness where he remained with the wild beast. He was constantly tempted by the devil, but was also ministered to by the angels. After returning from Jordan, and prior to being led into the wilderness by the spirit, Jesus was full of the Holy Ghost (Luke 4:1KJV).

For forty days, Jesus fasted in the wilderness,(Matthew4:2 Luke 4:2KJV) and at the end was very hungry . From past experience, the devil seems to wait until we are the weakest, whether from sickness, financial, emotional problems or from fasting, to try to take advantage. This could be what happened to Jesus. Having gone without any type of food for forty days and nights (Matthew 4:2; Luke 4:2KJV) could make the body weak. Jesus was in human form at this time (Matthew 4:3-4; Luke 4:3-4KJV). Both scriptures tell us that the tempter (devil) came to Jesus and said, "If thou be he Son of God, command these stones be made bread."(Matthew 4:4, Luke 4:4KJV) Jesus told the devil, "man shall not live by bread alone, but by every word of God" (Mt. 4:4, Luke 4:4KJV).

Having failed in tempting Jesus, the devil tempted him a second time(Matthew 4:5, Luke 4:4KJV) by bringing him to Jerusalem (Mt. 4:5; Luke. 4:4KJV), and set him on a Pinnacle of the temple, estimated to be about 700 feet above the Kedron Valley or about half the height of the Empire State Building in New York he tempted him by saying, "If Thou be the Son of God, cast thy self down from hence".(Matthew 4:6, Luke 4:10-11KJV) The devil was trying to coerce Jesus into committing suicide in the pretense that if he really was who he claimed to be, angels would be ordered to look after him (Mt. 4:6; Luke 4:10-11KJV). Jesus responded by saying, "Thou shalt not tempt the Lord thy God" (Matthew 4:7; Luke 4:12KJV).

The devil, having been defeated twice,Matthew 4:8-9, Luke 4:5-7KJV) tried again with things of the world. The devil has a pretty good track record with this gimmick. Taking Jesus high up on a mountain, he showed him all the kingdoms of the world and promised him all the glory and power if he would only worship him (Mt, 4:8-9; Lk. 4:5-7). Once again the devil was defeated when Jesus told him, "Thou shall worship the

Lord thy God and him only." (Matthew 4:10, Luke 4:8KJV) Jesus then ordered Satan to get behind him (Matthew 4:10; Luke. 4:8KJV).

Having been ordered to get out of his life, the devil departed for a season (Luke. 4:13KJV), and the angels came and ministered unto Jesus (Matthew4:11KJV). Somewhere around this time, Herod, governor of the province had John the Baptist arrested and put in prison for telling Herodias, the wife of his brother Phillip, that it was not right for him to have this woman. It is believed that John was imprisoned in the fortress of Machaerus in Perea.

Herod wanted to kill John for what he had said, but was afraid of the people, since they all thought he was a prophet. However, during Herod's birthday celebrations, Herodias daughter, Salome, the daughter of Phillip and Herodias, delighted him by dancing before his guests, so much that he swore to give her anything she liked. All she had to do was ask. Salome, prompted by her mother said, "I want you to give me, here and now, on a dish, the head of John the Baptist."(Matthew 14:8KJV). Herod was aghast at this request, but because he had sworn in front of his guests, he gave orders that she should be given what she had asked for. Herod sent men and had John beheaded in the prison. Then his head was carried in on a dish and presented to the young girl who handed it to her mother.

Later John's disciples came, took the body of John the Baptist and buried it. Then, they went and told the news to

Jesus.

Having heard about this, Jesus went into Galilee preaching the gospel of the kingdom of God. His message was, "The Time is Full Filled, and The Kingdom of God Is At Hand; repent ye and believe the gospel" (Mark1:14-15KJV).

Jesus not only taught and preached in the synagogues of Galilee, but he healed all manner of sickness and disease (Matthew 23-24; Matthew 8:16; 9:35KJV). Herod, the governor who had ordered the death of John The Baptist, heard all the reports about Jesus and said to his men, "This must be John the Baptist: he has risen from the dead. That is why miraculous powers are at work in him" (Matthew 14:12KJV).

Healings By Jesus

A Leper (Matthew 8:1-3; Mark1:40-42; Luke 5:12 KJV)

Centurion's Palsied Servant Matthew 8:5-13; Luke 7:1-10 KJV)

Peter's Mother-In-Law (Matthew 8:14-15; Mark 1:29-31; Luke 4:38-40 KJV)

Devil Possessed & Divers Disease (Matthew 8:16; Mark 1:32-34; Luke 4:40-41 KJV)

Two Maniacs of Gergesa (Matthew 8:28-34 KJV)

Bed-ridden Palsy Victim (Matthew 9:1-7; Mark2:1-12; Luke 5:18 KJV)

Woman with Issue of Blood (Matthew 9:20-22; Mark 5-25-

34; Luke 8:43 KJV)

Jairus' Daughter (Matthew 9:18, 19, 23-25; Mark 5:21, 24, 35 KJV)

Two Blind Men (Matthew 9:27-31 KJV)

Devil Possessed Dumb Man (Matthew 9:32-34 KJV)

Withered Hand Healed on Sabbath (Matthew 12:9-13; Mark 3:1-5; Lark6:6-11 KJV)

Multitudes Healed (Matthew 12:15; Mark 3:7-12; Luke6-17-19 KJV)

Blind and Dumb Healed (Matthew 12:22-23; Luke 11:14 KJV)

Multitudes(Matthew 14:14; Luke 9:11 KJV)

People of Gennesaret (Matthew 14:34-36; Mark 6:53-56 KJV)

Syrophenician Woman's Daughter (Matthew 15:21-28; Mark 7:24-30 KJV)

Lame-Blind-Dumb-Maimed-Many Others (Matthew 29-31; Mark 7:31-37 KJV)

Lunatick and Vexed Boy (Matthew 17:14-18; Mark 9:17-27; Luke 9:38 KJV)

Multitudes Healed (Matthew 1:1-2 KJV)

Two Blind Men (Matthew 20:29-34KJV)

Blind and Lame (Matthew 21:14KJV)

Maniac of Gadara (Mark 5:1-16; Luke 8:26-39 KJV)

Blind Man (Mark 8:22-26KJV)

Blind Bar-ti-mae-us (Mark 10:46-52; Luke 18:35-43 KJV)

Widows Son (Luke 7:11-15 KJV)

Woman Loosened From Satan (Luke 13:10-17 KJV)

Man With Dropsy Healed on Sabbath (Luke 14:1-6 KJV)

Ten Lepers (Luke 17:11-19 KJV)

High Priest's Servants Ear Cut off (Luke 22:51 KJV)

Nobleman's Son (John 4:46-54 KJV)

Man with Infirmity for 38 years (John 5:1-15 KJV)

Blind Man at Pool of Si-lo-am (John 9:1-7 KJV)

FIRST SERMON OF JESUS

Having returned from the wilderness, Jesus came to Nazareth where he had been brought up.(Luke 4:16KJV) Upon entering the synagogue, he stood up to read (Luke 4:16KJV).

It was customary, on each sabbath, for seven persons to read. A priest, a Levite and five ordinary Israelites. It was also the custom, out of respect to God and his word, that all readers of the Scripture stand while reading (1 King 8:14, 22; Nehemiah 8:4-7; 9:2-4KJV).

The prophetic books were in single volumes with the exception of the twelve minor prophets. Having been given the book of the Prophet Esaias, Greek form of Isaiah, Jesus opened it and found the place where it was written that the Spirit of the Lord was upon him and he had the anointing to preach the gospel to the poor, heal the broken hearted, preach deliverance to the captives, recovering sight to the blind and set at liberty them that are bruised (Luke 4:17-18KJV). This message from Jesus was the fulfilling of Old Testament prophecy (Isaiah 61:1-2KJV).

Having completed his message, Jesus closed the book, gave it to the minister and sat down. While everyone in the congregation were looking at him, Jesus spoke again. "This day is the scripture fulfilled in your ears". (Luke 4:21).

The congregation was awe struck and someone asked, "is this not the son of Joseph"? (John 6:42KJV).Jesus had got their attention, but in doing so had stirred up a hornets nest.

As Jesus continued talking or preaching, as some might say in olden days lingo, busting their hides, he talked about Elijah and Elisha whom were considered to be of the greatest of Prophets. The people became filled with wrath when Jesus, the "hometown boy:, placed himself in the same class as these prophets and referred to Gods' blessing the heatheren whom were despised and considered unworthy of sharing in the divine power.

What did the congregation do about this "hide busting radical upstart" as some probably referred to him being?

I can't help wonder if it was the head deacon, members of the pastors council or some political self-proclaimed religious leader that led the pack, but whomever, the congregation rose up and not only threw Jesus out of the city, but took him to the brow of a hill, that was estimated to be about forty feet high, where Nazareth was built, and intended to cast him down headlong (Luke 4:28-29KJV), like Judas fell headlong (Acts 1:18KJV).

Is it possible that this crowd was so worked up that they

intended to hang Jesus? I wonder what would happen to some ministers today if they started preaching the truth in their churches, instead of preaching what the congregation wants to hear?

Jesus was able to escape through the midst of the riled up church folks and went on his way (Luke 4:30KJV).

Jesus was never really successful in his home-town (Matthew 13:53-58; Mark 6:1-5KJV), and offended many by his remarks (Mark 6:3KJV). Jesus said unto them, "A prophet is not without honor, but in his own country, and among his own kin, and in his own house" (Mark 6:4KJV).

The fame of Jesus went through all Syria, a district of ten cities, and the residents brought all the sick people to Jesus for healing. Some of the afflicted were possessed with devils, lunatics, had palsy, divers diseases, and torments.

Jesus would have had a great time had he visited the nations capitol. With all the devils and lunatics, disguised as elected officials, Jesus could have spent his entire ministry there casting out devils and cleaning up the corruption. President Trump claims he is going to drain the swamp, but he needs to be careful or some of the Political demons may jump on him.

All the folks that were brought to Jesus for healing, he healed them (Matthew 4:24KJV). Jesus became a very popular figure and possible was the first traveling evangelist, moving from city to city (Matthew 9:35KJV) and about the villages (Mark 6:6KJV). As news spread about his "miracle crusades",

Jesus was moved with compassion of the multitudes because they fainted and were scattered abroad (Matthew 9:36KJV). In some instances, the crowds were innumerable in so much that they trode one upon another (Luke 12:1KJV). One writer suggests that the crowds could have been in the hundreds of thousands; larger than President Trump's crowds.

Many preachers, like the former pastor of the Hillside Covenant Church in Conn., featured some of the state's top country music bands to draw a crowd, while other preachers use tents and various type gimmicks to attract people. Jesus did it the old fashion way; preaching the word of God. Wonder what would happen if all the preachers were like the Swaggart family and their singers?

Naturally everyone was not happy about the success and popularity of Jesus. Things usually run pretty smooth until the government tries to take over. Jesus had the same problem. Maybe the government thought Jesus was not paying all his taxes or maybe they were just jealous. In any case, on more than one occasion, when Jesus was in the temple teaching, the chief priests and elders of the people came unto him and wanted to know by what authority he was doing these things and who gave him his authority (Matthew 21:23; Mark11:27-28; Luke 20:1-2KJV).

Knowing politics, it is possible they were concerned whether Jesus had bought a business license or a permit from the chamber of commerce to preach on the street or in the temples.

In response to their interrogation, Jesus confused and humiliated them by answering them with a question concerning John the Baptist (Matthew 21:24-27; Mark 11-27-33; Luke 20:3-7KJV) and making them appear more ridiculous by his answer concerning the resurrection (Matthew 22:23-33; Mark 12:18-27; Luke 20:27-38KJV).

Most politicians become confused with facts and truth. More than likely, the chief priests and elders built up more hatred of Jesus. The "I'll get even devil" probably entered them at this time.

JESUS CHOOSES DISCIPLES

Having served in banking for eleven years and elected Mayor of Talladega, Alabama for four terms, I am aware of the importance of selecting individuals for position of trust. Every effort must be made to choose a person that will be trustworthy, dependable, honest, devoted and loyal to the employer and or administration. The late President Nixon, President Clinton and President Donald Trump are very aware of the need to select individuals and vet them properly to help insure they will not create a problem. By not doing an extensive background check of proposed cabinet members could be problematic for the administration. President Nixons and Clintons administration were plagued with members going to prison and even one allegedly committed suicide. President Trump is experiencing some of the same problem early on in his presidency.

In considering a person to be a disciple, a representative of Jesus, one would think that an even more rigid vetting or investigation would be in order. What type background check did Jesus do in choosing his disciples? Were they checked for trustworthiness, honest Christian principles or did Jesus know every thing without checking? If this be true, why would he choose men like Peter who denied him and Judas who betrayed him? At one time, all the disciples forsook Jesus and fled (Matthew26:56KJV). Reminds me of politics. When things are going good, there are many friends. However, let a little controversy happen and friends are hard to find.

We know that Jesus does not know all things. Matthew 24:36;Mark 13:32; Acts 1:7KJV) Only God knows when Jesus will return to earth (Matthew 24:36; Mark 13:32; Acts 1:7KJV). However, Jesus knew who would betray him (John 6:64KJV).

Since the writings of John were more than fifty years later than the writings of Matthew, is it possible Jesus did not know Judas would betray him at the time of him being chosen a disciple, but being revealed later on?

Is it fair to compare the choosing of disciples to hiring an employee, selecting a pastor or making a political appointment? At first thought, one might say, Jesus was not a political figure. It is true Jesus never served in an elected or appointed position, but whether by design or destiny, Jesus stirred up a lot of controversy. Some of the issues were like we have today. Had Jesus been preaching and teaching today, wonder how he would have handled issues like, tithe paying, wife swapping, legalizing marijuana, swingers clubs, distribution of wealth, reparation, abortion, same sex marriage, school prayer, AIDS issue, homosexuality, gambling, sexual discrimination, voting rights and all the multitude of moral issues that have placed the church and government at odds?

His critics, the lawyers, scribes, elders and chief priests were constantly trying to destroy him (Matthew 12-14; Luke. 6-11; 19:47KJV). Not a lot has changed over the years. Some of these same type people are still trying to tear our country apart. Hardly a day passes that we don't read or see in the news where some religious group has claimed responsibility for bombings or beheading of Americans in the name of their god.

There is not really any information why Jesus made his choice or how, but many of the disciples seemed to be unlikely characters.

The names of the twelve were, Simon, who was called Peter, his brother Andrew, James the son of Zebedee and John his brother, Phillip and Bartholomew, Thomas and Matthew the publican, James the son of Alphaeus and Lebbaeus whose surname was Thaddaeus, Simon the Canaanite and the last being Judas Iscariot, son of Simon (Matthew 10:2-4KJV). Of the twelve, Judas Iscariot died at the time Jesus was sentenced to death.

The mission of these twelve was limited to the Jews (Matthew 10:5-6KJV). The Jews then and now make up all the tribes of Israel (Matthew 19:28; Acts 26:7; James 1:1; Revelations 7:4; 21:12KJV).

While Simon was the first disciple chosen, (Matthew 10:2; Mark 3:16; Luke 6:14KJ), Andrew was following Jesus first and introduced his brother Peter to Jesus (John 1:35-42KJV). However, the scriptures seem to bear out that the two were chosen or called at the same time (Matthew 4:18-20; Mark 1:16-18; and Luke 5:11KJV).

Regardless of who was called in what order, with the exception of Judas, who was chosen last, I have chosen to list the names alphabetically.

ANDREW

The brother of Simon Peter, a native Palestinian Jew, and possible of the tribe of Reuben, was one of the first disciples chosen by Jesus. Andrew, the son of Bar-Jona (Matthew 16:17KJV), aramic for :"son of Jonah" or Jona (John 1:42; 21:15-17, bore a good Greek name. As a resident of Bethsaida in Galilee (John 1:44; 12:21KJV), his life was strongly influenced by Gentile culture. Andrew spoke Greek as well s Aramic.

As a professional fisherman of the Sea of Galilee (Matthew 4:18KJV), Andrew not only lived with Peter in Capernaum (Mark 1:21KJV), but they worked in partnership with the sons of Zebedee, James and John (Luke 5:10KJV).

When John the Baptist was preaching at Bethany, (KJV "Beh-abara") beyond the Jordan (Matthew 31:1; Luke 3:3; John 1:8KJV), Andrew, like many of his countrymen, laid aside his daily work to go hear the famous preacher. What Andrew saw and heard influenced him greatly. He not only became a disciple of John (John 1:35- 40KJV), but received John's baptism of repentance and committed himself to receive the

Messiah when he came.

When John the Baptist pointed out Jesus as "the Lamb of God", Andrew and another disciple, possible John, acted upon the implied suggestion of the Baptist and sought an interview with Jesus. This interview convinced Andrew that Jesus was indeed the expected Messiah (John1:35-42KJV), and thus became one of he first acknowledged followers of Jesus.

Andrew enthusiastically went in search of his brother Simon to share the discovery with him. He used his good influence to bring him to personal contact with Jesus (John 1:40-42KJV). It is believed Andrew was traveling with Jesus when he found Phillip and Jesus told Phillip, "Follow Me" (John 1:43KJV). I am also of the opinion that Andrew was with Jesus when he healed the son of the Nobleman (John. 4:46-54KJV).

Having been rejected at Nazareth, Jesus established his headquarters at Capernaum (Matthew 4:3; Mark 1:21-45; 2:1-6; 9:33; Luke 4:31; 7:1-10; John 4:46-53; 6:17-25, 59KJV) which is upon the sea coast in the borders of Zab-u-lon and Neph-Tha-lim (Matthew 4:13KJV). It is believed that this is the time that Jesus called Andrew, Peter, James and John into full time training to be "fishers of men (Matthew 4:18-22; Mark 1:16-20; Luke 5:1-11KJV). Andrew had already returned to Galilee and resumed his work as a fisherman.

Andrew was in all the lists of the Twelve (Matthew 10:2-4; Mark 3:16-19; Luke 6:14-16; Acts 1:13KJV), and was always named among the first four, although the order varies.

Andrew was associated with Peter, James and John in their 'private' inquiry of Jesus concerning his predictions of the future (Mark 13:3-4KJV). Andrew never attained the intimacy and resultant privileges of the other three as the "inner circle", but was always on the fringe of it.

In perplexity at the last Passover, Phillip conferred with Andrew concerning the request of some Greeks for an interview with Jesus. Andrew concluded that the solution was to lay the request before Jesus himself, and let him decide whether or not to grant the interview (John 12:20-22KJV).

Andrew's name is included among those who waited in the Upper Room after the Ascension of Jesus (Acts 1:13KJV). However, following that occasion, Andrew's name is omitted from the New Testament.

Tradition has been busy with the later life of Andrew. Eusebius Hist. III, records the tradition that Andrew's area of labor was in Scythia; hence he has been adopted as the patron saint of Russia. Other traditions connect him with Lydia, Thrace, and Achaia. The apocryphal Acts of Andrew picture him as evangelizing in Achair and being martyed at Patras by being bound to an Z-shaped cross, crux decussata, subsequently called St. Andrew's Cross. He has been made the patron saint of Greece. A later tradition claims that his body was transferred to Constantinople, and then to Italy during the Crusades. Andrew also has been made the patron saint of Scotland based on the late tradition that his arm was brought to the E coast by St. Regulus.

Only in the fourth gospel does the character of Andrew emerge with distinctioness. He was a sincere man with earnest and devout Meessianic expectations. He was not bound by traditional views, but was open to and eager for new truth. Andrew had the courage of his convictions, and was eager and enthusiastic to have others share what he had come to know. He was always busy bringing others into touch with his Master. As a man of action, he was practical, ready and willing to do any needed task. He has been called the first home missionary (John 1:41KJV) as well as the first foreign missionary.

Andrew did not possess the native ability and aggressive leadership of his brother Peter and was content to play a lesser role. His broad sympathies, practical common sense, and steady discipleship made him a valuable member of the apostolic band.

We need more men like Andrew in church and politics!!!!!!!!!!!!!!!!

JAMES

V ery little is known and written about this disciple who is listed ninth in Luke's list of the apostles (Luke 6:14 KJV)

A son of Alphaeus . (Matthew10:3,Mark 3:18, Luke 6:15, Acts 1:13 KJV) and Mary (Mark 15:40,16:1; Luke 24:10KJV) he was a brother to Judas......not Iscariot (Luke 6:16, Acts 1:13 KJV), Matthew and Simon Zealots (Luke 6:15 KJV). This James was not the half brother of Jesus (Acts 1:13-14 KJV). James also had another brother named Joses (Matthew 27:56;Mark 15:47 KJV) and possibly a sister named Salome (Mark 16:1 KJV).

Depending on the interpretation, Salome could be the sister of James or the wife of Zebedee. This verse says, and when the sabbath was passed, Mary Magdalene and Mary, the mother of James and Salome had bought sweet spices that they might come and anoint him. Although not an apostle, Joses must have been well known because his name is mentioned several times in the scriptures.

The mother of James was the sister of the mother of Jesus

(John 19:25KJV), and the wife of Cleophas, who was also called Alpheus (Mat 10:3; Mark3:18; (Luke 6:15 KJV).

It is apparent that the mother of James and Joses was a very devoted follower of Jesus. She was an eye witness to the crucifixion and one of the women who came to prepare the body of Jesus for burial. (Mark16:1 KJV)

James is very obscure and his prominence is reflected in his nickname as being James the Less (Mark 15:40 KJV). The Greek word for Less is micros, meaning little. The primary meaning is small in statue. This could be referring to his features as short or small-framed man.

Apparently James was not a man who sought the lime light. He displayed no great leadership or asked the critical questions and his life and work is hidden in obscurity, but was still a disciple who Jesus trained and gave him all the powers as the other eleven.

Historians are divided about the ministry of James the less. Some say he took the gospel to Syria and Persia as well as other places. The way he died is as disputed. Some say he was stoned; others say he was beaten to death and others say he was crucified like Jesus.

JAMES

J ames, a son of Zebedee, was not only the older brother of John the apostle, but a cousin of Jesus. James, John and Zebedee were professional fishermen who were in business with Simon Peter and his brother Andrew (Luke 5:10 KJV). Jesus surnamed James and John, "Boanerges", meaning "son of thunder" (Mark. 3:17 KJV).

James and John wanted to be a part of the glory of Jesus (Mark 10-37 KJV), and requested they be permitted to sit on each side of him. The other ten disciples were upset over this request, and Jesus had to settle the squabble (Matthew 20:24; Mark 10:41-45 KJV).

James, John and Peter were some of the favorite disciples of Jesus. On more than on occasion, these three were chosen to go with Jesus to pray, heal the sick or raise the dead (Mark 5:37; 9:2; 14:33; Luke 8:51; 9:28 KJV).

Tradition says James was of the tribe of Levi through his father, and of Judah through his mother. They were not only religious but wealthy. Sounds like some of the cabinet members President Trump has chosen to be in his cabinet.

James preached in India with Peter and later in Spain. He became the Patron Saint of Spain.

King Herod agrippa, the son of Aristobulus, grandson of Herod the Great and nephew of Herod Antipas, who killed John the Baptist, stretched forth his hands to vex certain members of the church and killed James, the brother of John, with a sword (Acts 12:1-2 KJV). A person being killed by the sword was considered disgraced and the Jews were pleased (Acts 12:3 KJV).

James was the first apostle to suffer martyrdom.

JOHN

A son of Zebedee (Matthew 4:21 KJV), brother of James (Matthew 10:2; 17:1; Acts 12:2 KJV), was also a professional fisherman and was in business with his father and his brothers, Peter and Andrew (Luke 5:10 KJV).

Jesus surnamed John and James "Boanerges", (Mark 3:17 KJV) meaning "son of thunder" (Mark 3:17 KJV). These two wanted to be a part of the glory of Jesus (Mark10:37 KJV), and created a controversy by requesting they be permitted to sit on each side of him. The other ten disciples became upset and Jesus had to settle the squabble (Mark 10-41-45 KJV). Because of his boldness, John was perceived to be unlearned and ignorant (Acts 4:13 KJV).

Considered a pillar, the word being derived from the Greek word Stulos, is a word used by the Jews of great teachers of the law and persons of importance. John had prominence among the apostles (Galations 2:9 KJV).

John was a peculiar person with low tolerance. His attitude was "if you aren't for me, then you are against me, so let's do away with you" (Mark 9:38; Luke 9:49-56 KJV). The attitude of

John reminds one of President Donald Trump.

It is obvious that John was among the favorite disciples of Jesus. Having being chosen to go with Jesus to pray, heal the sick and raise the dead (Mark 5:37; 9:2; 14:33;Luke 8:51; 9:28 KJV), Jesus chose John and Peter to prepare the Passover, known as the Last Supper (Luke 22:8-13 KJV).

The scriptures do not refer to John by name, but it is believed that he, along with Peter, followed Jesus into the high palace of the high priest following the arrest of him (John 18:15-18); at the crucifixion (John 19:26 KJV); at the tomb (John 20:2-8 KJV), and was placed in jail for preaching (Acts 4:1-3; 5:18 KJV).

John was banished to one of the Sporades islands in the Mediterranean, Aegean Sea, called Patmos (Revelations 1:9 KJV), for preaching the word of God and testifying of Jesus Christ. I wonder how many preachers would preach the word of God if they were threatened with jail or death?

The island of Patmos, located thirty seven miles w.s.w. of Miletus, consists of volcanic hills and is treeless and rocky. It is estimated that Patmos is ten miles long from n-s and it's greatest width being six miles at the north end. Patmos is located thirty miles southwest of samos. The romans used such small islands as places of political exile (TAC. ANN. 3.68; 4:30; 15:71 KJV). Allegedly, the lowest of criminals were placed here and forced to do hard labor. Ancient Christian tradition. reported e.g., by Eusebius Hist. III. 18.1, states that John was banished to Patmos by the Emperor Domitian in A.D. 95.

It is believed that John survived being boiled in burning oil and was released eighteen months later when Nerva became emperor III. 20.8-9) John supposedly died a natural death at age 100.

The monastery of Saint John, founded by Christodulos in A.D. 1088, is located near the traditional "cave of revelation".

John is the author of the gospel Epistles 1,2,3 and John and Revelation.

MATTHEW

One day, Jesus was out walking in Capernaum, when he saw a man named Matthew, sitting at the tax receipt of common, (tax collectors post), and Jesus said to Matthew,(Matthew 9:9KJV) who was the son of Alphaeus, "Follow Me". (Matthew 9:9KJV) Without any question, Matthew got up and began to walk with Jesus (Matthew 9:9KJV).

Matthew was a Publican, not a Republican, and a 1st-century Galilean, possible being born in Galilee, which was not a part of Judea or the Roman Judaea province. Being a Roman Tax Collector (Matthew. 9:9; 10:3; Mark 2:13-14; Luke 5:27KJV), he would have been literate in Aramaic and Greek. Tax collectors were held in disrepute and anyone serving in this position was despised by the Jews and considered in the same class as sinners. They had the reputation of being extortionists and cheating the public. Matthew would have been right at home in American politics.

As a tax-gatherer, Matthew sat in the custom house and since this job did not pay a salary, the tax-gatherers levied the amount of tax on each one as prescribed by the Roman Government and always added a little extra for themselves.

Several days later after Jesus had asked Matthew to follow him, Jesus and his disciples were sitting in Matthew's house having a meal with many Scribes and Pharisees, AKA tax collectors and sinners (Matthew 9:10 KJV).

Whomever it was, someone leaked it to the Pharisees about Jesus associating with these undesirables and they asked the disciples, "Why does your master eat with Publicans and sinners?" (Matthew 9:11 KJV). This leaking of the news and the questioning of the disciples, reminds me of modern day news reporters. Looking for a story and stirring up a stink.

Sometime later when Jesus learned about what had been said, He told his disciples that they who are not sick does not need a doctor, but those who are sick need a doctor (Matthew 9:12 KJV). Jesus continued saying that He had not come to call the righteous; but sinners to repentance (Matthew 9:13 KJV).

The name "Matthew" means "gift of the Lord". In Mark and Luke telling about the calling of Matthew, they refer to Matthew as "Levi". Some suggest Jesus gave him a new name when Matthew became a follower of Him, but other writers think Matthew could have been a member of the tribe of Levi.

After Pentecost, the scriptures are silent about the life of Matthew. However, different writers like Irenaeus and Clement of Alexandria, claim that Matthew preached the gospel to the Jewish community in Judea before traveling to other countries.

Church historian Eusebius (260-340 C.E.) says that Matthew collected the oracles, logia: sayings of or about Jesus in the Hebrew language and then translated the sayings as best as possible.

Matthew is recognized as a saint in the Roman Catholic, Eastern Orthodox, Lutheran and Anglican churches. His feast day is celebrated on 21 September in the West and 16 November in the East.

The Roman Catholic Church and the Orthodox Church hold to the tradition that Matthew dies a martyr. However, this belief has been rejected by the gnostic heretic Heracleon as early as the second century.

NATHANEAL

Nathanael, also known as Bartholomew, and being referred to as "Son of Tomai" was a brother of Phillip. "Son of Tomai" is an uncommon name for males and a unique surname for all people from the Aramaic. It also has a meaning of son of furrows, perhaps meaning ploughman.

Before accepting the call to be a disciple, Nathanael questioned Phillip about Jesus and wanted to know if anything good could come out of Nazareth. Phillip responded by saying, "Come and see." (John 1:46 KJV)

One writer describes Nathanael, AKA Bartholomew, as having black curly hair that covered his ears, a long grizzled middle height beard, white skin, large eyes, and a straight nose. It is said that he wore a white robe with a purple stripe and a white cloak with four purple gems at the corners. For twenty six-years he wore these and it is said that they never grew old. It is further stated that his shoes lasted as long as his clothes.

Historians claim that Nathanael/Bartholomew prayed a hundred times a day and a hundred times at night. His voice sounded like a trumpet, angels waited upon him and that he was always cheerful and knew all the languages of the times.

When Jesus saw Nathanael coming toward him, he said, "Behold an Israelite indeed, in whom is no guile.(John1:47-48 KJV) "Nathanael responded by saying, "Whence knowest thou me?" Jesus responded that he saw him under the fig tree before Phillip called him. Nathanael responded, "Rabbi, thou are the Son of God: thou are the King of Israel." (John 1:47-48 KJV)

Phillip not only was from Cana where Jesus performed his first miracle of turning water into wine at the wedding feast (John 21:2; John 2:1-11 KJV), but along with Jude (Thaddaeus) was the first to evangelize among the Armenians throughout the years of 43 to 66 AD. Phillip joined Bartholomew and they traveled to Asia Minor and labored in Hierapolis, near Laodicea and Colosse in what is now referred to as Turkey. Another writer believes Nathanael preached in Syria, Phrygia and India.

While in Hierapolis, theologians claim the the wife of the Roman proconsul, a government official, was healed by the apostles Phillip and Bartholomew and she became a christian. Because of this, her husband, King Astyages ordered them to be put to death by crucifixion. Phillip was crucified but for some reason, Bartholomew was ordered to be taken down from the cross and be dismissed. From there, he went eastward to India, the area around the Caspian Sea and then to Armenia. It is there he was allegedly tied up and stretched out on a specifically-designed torture device and a sharp knife was used to remove the outer skin, then hung on a cross up side down where he died.

It is said that he converted Polymius, the King of Armenia to Christianity. It is ironic that Polymius's brother Astyages, is the one who ordered the gruesome execution of Bartholomew.

In the 13th century, Saint Bartholomew Monastery was a prominent Armenian monastery constructed at the site of the martyrdom of Apostle Bartholomew in the Vaspurakan Province of Greater Armenia, now in southeastern Turkey.

PETER

S imon, having been renamed Peter by Jesus (Mark 3:16; Luke 6:14; John 1:42 KJV), and being Greek meaning "a rock", was also called Cephas (John 1:42 KJV), which being aramaic for "rock" (John 1:42 KJV).

Peter, a sword carrier (Jn. 18:10), was a resident of Bethsaida (John 1:44 KJV), a city and a desert place by the sea of Galilee. Bethsida was also the home of several other apostles (John 1:44; John 12:21 KJV).

Peter, a man that acted without thinking, would have fit in perfectly with local politics or some churches of today. Because of his boldness, Peter was perceived to be unlearned and ignorant (Acts 4:13 KJV).

Peter was a son of Jonah (Matthew 16:17; John 1:42 KJV), and a fisherman by trade and was in business with his brother Andrew and father. Even though being from Bethsaida (John 1:44 KJV), they resided in Capernaum, the headquarters of Jesus.

Peter was married (Mark 1:30; 1 Corinthians 9:5 KJV), owned his house in Capernaum (Mark 1:29 KJV) whom he shared with his mother-in-law (Mark 1:30 KJV). His brother, Andrew, also lived with him (Mark 1:29 KJV).

Peter held the position of leadership within the ranks of the disciples. His name is listed in the four lists of the twelve disciples in the N.T. (Mark 10:2; Mark 3:16; Luke 6:14-16; and in Acts 1:13 KJV). In the gospels, Peter is the most frequently mentioned of the twelve and was the spokesman for them on many occasions (Matthew 15:15; 16:16; 18:21; 19:27 Mark 8:29; 10:28; Luke 9:20; 12:41; and 18:28 KJV). Peter being approached by the Temple tax collectors is another indication of his leadership role (Matthew 17:24 KJV).

Having been approached by the tax collector, Jesus ordered Peter to go fish and take up the fish that first cometh up(Matthew 17:27 KJV), open the mouth of the fish and remove the piece of money and pay the taxes (Matthew 17:27 KJV). It is believed that this piece of money was the equivalent of .64 cents.

There are four occasions recorded in the gospels, in which the inner circle of the disciples are alone with Jesus. The inner circle included Peter, James and John, sons of Zebedee. On one occasion, Andrew was included (Mark 13:3 KJV), and during this meeting, Peter asked Jesus about his return to earth.

When Jesus raised the daughter of Jairus from the dead, He took Peter, James and John into the room (Mark 5:37; Luke 8:51 KJV). These three also witnessed the Transfiguration of Jesus (Matthew 17:1-9); Mark 9:2-10; Luke 9:28-36 KJV).

During his agonizing experience in Gethsemane, Jesus took Peter, James and John with him into the garden (Matthew 26:37; Mark 14:33 KJV). It is at this time that Jesus gave Peter a tongue lashing for sleeping instead of keeping watch (Matthew 26:40; Mark 14:37 KJV). While all the disciples went to sleep, only Peter was singled out for the rebuke. This was another example of his role as a leader of and spokesman for the disciples (Matthew 26:40; Mark 14:37 KJV).

Wonder how many so called Christians or religious leaders are like Peter, James and John who are sleeping when they should be praying and watching? No question that Peter was a man of contrasts, especially in the gospels. Peter was not always stable and reliable as his name implied.

Following his splendid confession at Caesarea Philippi, Peter objected violently to Jesus' predictions regarding his passion. This prompted Jesus' strong rebuke. Get behind me, Satan! You are a hindrance to me; for you are not on the side of God, but of men" (Matthew 16:23; Mark 8:33 KJV). This was a striking benediction of Jesus(Matthew 16: 17-18 KV).

Another demonstration of his erratic trait is when he attempted to walk on water(Matthew 14:28-31 KJV). Peter began with a bold declaration of faith, but the swelling waves frightened him. Having rescued him, Jesus rebuked him by saying, "O man of little faith, why did you doubt?" (Matthew 14:31 KJV)

At the foot washing in the Upper Room, Peter protested

and said, "Thou shall never wash my feet" (John 13:6-8 KJV). However, Peter changed his mind when Jesus said, " If I wash thee not, thou hast no part with me" (John 13:8-9 KJV). Peter responded by saying, "Lord, not only my feet, but also my hands and my head" (John 13:9 KJV).

On the way to the Mount of Olives, Peter protested strongly that Jesus had made the statement that all his followers would abandon him. Peter pledged his loyalty to the utmost (Matthew 26:33; Mark 14:29; Luke 22:33; John 13:37 KJV). Jesus responded with the somber prediction that Peter would deny him (Matthew 26:30-35; Mark 14:26-31; Luke 22:31-34; John 13:36-38 KJV).

Just as Jesus had predicted, later on in the evening, before the cock crew three times, Peter denied knowing Jesus, three times, nor having any association with "the Galilean"(Matthew 26:69-75; Mark 14:66-72; Luke 22:54-62; John 18:25-27 KJV). While the accounts of this being recorded four times, Matthew and Mark reports that Peter supported his third denial by invoking a curse on himself and by swearing (Matthew 26:74: Mark 14:71 KJV.) As the cock began crowing, Peter was brought to his senses. The confident boasts of Peter earlier that night, were meaningless when he faced danger and harm by his association with Jesus. It was at this time that all the disciples tucked tail and ran (Matthew 26:56 KJV). Does this remind one of closet followers of Jesus? As long as some so called Christians don't have to take a public stand, they are okay, but when there is a prayer day being held at the court house grounds or other locations, it is hard to get the preachers to show up in support. The newspapers or TV stations might be there and expose them.

Later on that night, his encounter with Jesus in the courtyard, of the house of Caiaphas, must have been heart wrenching as the Lord turned and looked at Peter. (Lk. 22:61). Peter went out and wept bitterly (Matthew 26:75; Luke 22:62 KJV). Unlike Judas, Peter did repent. Peter had a faith in Jesus that could be renewed; Judas did not.

Even though Peter had his problems, he did display a flash of bravery, although misguided, when he cut off the ear of Malchus (John 18:10 KJV), the high priest's servant (Matthew 26:52-54; Mark. 14:47; Luke 22:49-51 KJV;)

In the early history of the church, Peter displayed vital leadership. Shortly after the Ascension, Peter presided over the appointment of a replacement of Judas Iscariot (Acts 1:15-26 KJV). Peter boldly addressed the crowds on Pentecost Sunday and his sermon was instrumental in the conversion of about three-thousand (Acts 2:41 KJV). After Pentecost, Peter miraculously healed a lame man at the Beautiful Gate of the Temple (Acts 3:1-10 KJV). Peter was the spokesman in the episode involving Ananias and Sapphira when they lied to the Holy Ghost about their land transaction (Acts 5:1-11 KJV). They both dropped dead. This is the first recorded sin and its results in the early church. Peter also performed miracles of healing in Lydda and in Joppa (Acts 9:32-34; Acts 9:36-43

KJV). Peter preached another sermon which led to the arrest of him and John (Acts 3:11-26; Acts 4:1-4 KJV). The next morning after their arrest, Peter, who had been filled with the Holy Ghost (Acts 2:4 KJV), spoke impressively in court (Acts 4:5-22 KJV). Having received the Holy Ghost, gave Peter more boldness and less fear of man and what they could do to him. Jesus says,(Matthew 10:28, Luke 12:4-5 KJV) "Fear not them which kill the body, but are not able to kill the soul: but rather fear him which is able to destroy both soul and body in hell" (Matthew 10-28; Luke 12:4-5 KJV).

In an outburst of persecution, Herod killed James, the brother of John and immediately imprisoned Peter (Acts 12:1-20; Acts 12:3-5 KJV). However, that night Peter was miraculously freed by an angel and Peter reported to the believers who were gathered at the house of Mary, in fervent prayer for his deliverance (Acts 12:6-11 KJV).

Upon arrival at the house where the prayer vigil was being held, when they saw Peter, they did not believe it was really him (Acts 12:13-16 KJV). Is this like some Christians of today? We ask God to intervene, but don't really believe he will while in many cases he already has.

After leaving the prayer meeting, Peter "went to another place" (Acts 12:17 KJV). Another example that had this happened today, with Peter being let out of jail by an angel, and the powers that be not knowing where he went, the folks at the prayer meeting could have been charged with conspiracy for shielding Peter from the government when in reality they did not know where Peter went. Today, when we read the scriptures about this event, we still do not know where Peter went.

It is believed that Peter was crucified head-downward (John. 21:18-19 KJV). The location of the tomb and the identification of his bones have been extensively debated in the 20th century. One writer, A.de Marco, did a full annotated bibliography entitled, The Tomb of St. Peter, 1964.

On June 26, 1968, Pope Paul VI, announced that the bones of Peter, had been positively identified by Margherita Garducci, who claimed to have located the bones in a marble chest, found in "Wall G", buried under St. Peter's Church in the Vatican.

While his bones remains a mystery, based on John 21: 16,19 KJVand John 21:18-19 KJV, there is no question that Peter spent the latter part of his life at Rome and died a Martyr's death.

Though not faultless, his positive traits were many and his enthusiasm, devotion and boldness is inspiring and challenging and are worthy of emulation. However, his negative traits should be a warning that enthusiasm and devotion must be tempered by a balanced and informed perspective. Misdirected and superficial enthusiasm can be dangerous.

Peter was committed to Christ; ARE YOU?

PHILLIP

T he day following Peter having been chosen as a disciple, Jesus went into Galilee and found Phillip (John 1:43 KJV). The Greek name for Phillip means, "lover of horses".

Phillip, a resident of Bethesaida, introduced his brother Nathaniel, (Bartholomew) to Jesus (John 1:44; 1:45-49 KJV. Phillip was also the disciple whom Jesus asked about a place to purchase bread in order to feed the five thousand (John 6:5-7 KJV). Is it possible that Jesus could have been testing the faith of Phillip?

It strongly suggested and believed that Phillip was from the tribe of Aebulaun and probably the first disciple of John The Baptist.

According to one tradition received from Clement of Alexandria (Strom. iii. 4, 25; iv. 9,73), Phillip was the one who asked permission to bury his father before following Jesus (Matthew 8:21; Luke 9:59 KJV). This cannot be proven by the scriptures.

Phillip is portrayed as a naive, rather shy but sober-minded person and probably received his Greek name in honor of

Phillip the Tetrach (Luke 3:1 KJV). This could be why the Greeks, who came to the Passover, sought him out on Palm Sunday as mediator between them and Christ (John 12:20-23 KJV).

Although reluctant to believe whole-heartedly in the kingdom because he failed to understand it, amid defective knowledge and imperfect spiritual insight, Phillip acquired a true missionary spirit and was instrumental in leading others to Christ. Phillip was among those in the Upper Room awaiting the coming of the Holy Spirit (Acts 1:13 KJV).

Historian Eusebius declares that Phillip is buried at Hierapolis along with his two virgin daughters. It is unclear how he died.

His relics are in the Church of the Apostles at Rome. In the Roman Church, his feast is celebrated May 1; in the Greek Church, November 14. His symbol is a cross with a loaf of bread on either side. This is in reference to where Phillip explains to Jesus that there was only two hundred pennyworth of bread and that would not be sufficient amount for the multitude to be fed (John 6:7 KJV). A pennyworth of bread would be about .17 cents, thus making the two hundred pennyworth of bread worth about $34.00.

SIMON

B eing called the Canaanite, an Aramic word for Zelotes, could indicate, before becoming a disciple, Simon might have been a member of some fanatical "zealot like" group in the Phinehas-Maccabean that rebelled against the Romans. History records that a multiplicity of such groups were active in Palestine during the first century A.D., and that these groups constituted an important part of the hard core of national resistance to Rome from the time of Pompey onward. There is no biblical evidence that actually links Simon with such an organization. (Matthew 10:4; Mark 3:18; Luke 6:15; Acts 1:13 KJV)

The theology of zeal which motivated the Zealot, originated in the exclusivistic worship of the true God of Israel: "I the Lord your God am a jealous God"(Exodus 20:5; 34:14; Deut. 4:24: 5:9; 6:15; Joshua 24:19; Ezekial 39:25 Zech 1:14: 8:2 KJV), and "Thou shalt have no other gods before me." (Exodus 20:3 KJV)

Israel was a holy people, and the law had been given to keep Israel holy unto God. Thus, when Israel excited God's jealousy by her apostasy, his wrath was poured upon his people. The propitiatory act of the Zealots was in a sense prophylactic. Like a surgeon excising a cancerous tissue, the Zealot extirpated the apostates from Israel with the sharp edge of the sword. The Zealot was the strict interpreter of the law, who was willing to follow the way of "zeal for the law of the God of Israel" unto death (Acts 22:4 KJV). The Zealot was willing not only to kill a Gentile, or to lay down his own life rather than transgress the law, but he was quite prepared to take the life of a fellow Israelite, if necessary, out of zeal for the law.

The theology of zeal was gradually circumscribed by the Jewish spiritual leaders after the crushing national defeats. In rabbinic Judaism, zeal was replaced by "shalom" as the dominant theological motif governing Israel's relations with the Gentiles.

In Christianity, zeal was redirected in terms consonant with the new theology (1 Corinthians 14:12; Titus 2:14; 1 Peter 3:13; Revelations 3:19 KJV)

Prior to his conversion, the Apostle Paul directly connected his activity as a persecutor of the church with zeal (Phil 3:6 KJV). Paul had been a Pharisee, but had gone beyond the requirements of this party in taking on the responsibilities of being a "zealot".

Jesus was remembered by his disciples to have acted like a "zealot" when he drove the money changers out of the temple:

Zeal for thine house hath eaten me up." (John 2:17; Ps. 69:9 KJV)

Tradition indicates Simon The Canaanite, was killed by crucifixion in Syria. One writer further indicates he could have been a brother of James, Matthew and Judas; not Iscariot.

However biblical evidence of this belief is unfounded.

THADDEAUS

Thaddaeus, one of the 12 Apostles, is believed that he was also known as Judas, son of James, not to be confused with Judas Iscariot, the man who betrayed Jesus. In some New Testament passages, the name Judas, son of James, appears instead. In ancient times, a person could have two or three different names, such as a Greek-language name and a Hebrew name, and in many cases, known primarily by their occupational title.

The name Thaddaeus is found only in the lists of the twelve apostles recorded in the first two gospels, Matthew 10:3; Mark 3:18 KJV, and in its place, Luke has Judas the son or brother of James (Luke 6:16; Acts 1:13 KJV). However, a man named Judas, son of James, is listed below Simon. In Luke 6:16 KJV, Judas, son of James, is listed again among the twelve Apostles, between Simon the Zealot and Judas Iscariot. In John 14:12 KJV, there is a reference to Judas, not Iscariot, who spoke to Jesus and asked him, "Lord, how is it that thou wilt manifest thyself unto us, and not unto the world?" However, these two names never appear in the same book, lending credence to the belief that they both refer to the same person. The"Gospel of the Ebionites," or "Gospel of the Twelve Apostles," of the 2nd century and mentioned by Origen, narrates that Thaddaeus was also among those who received their call to follow Jesus at the Sea of Tiberia, (Matthew 4:18-22 KJV).

In some of the scriptures, the word Apostle is used and also the word Disciple. An Apostle is an ambassador of the Gospel, basically a teacher. A Disciple is a pupil, a student, a follower, someone who was with Jesus the whole time he was on earth. The term apostle came to be exclusively used after the Ascension of Jesus. Peter in the Christian assembly gave the qualifications for an apostle as a preliminary to the choice of the replacement for Judas (Acts 1:21-22 KJV). While all apostles were disciples, not all disciples were apostles.

The unpopularity of the name "Judas" because of he treachery of Iscariot may have led to another name being used.

"Thaddaeus" is thought to have been derived from Aramaic, meaning the "breast-nipple." This might suggest that he was a character of almost feminine tenderness. Some Western manuscripts read "Lebbaeus" at Matthew 10:3. This is usually thought to be inauthentic and as probably derived from Hebrew leb,"courageous heart", explaining the name of "Thaddaeus."

If Judas is the same as Thaddaeus, he is not likely to be the brother of Jesus or the author of the epistle of Jude, though he may be the same as Judas, not Judas Iscariot of John 14:22. Jerome equates Thaddaeus, Lebbaeus, and Judas of James, and tells how he was sent on a mission to Abgar, king of Edessa.

Jude, also known as Judas Thaddaeus, Jude of James, Jude Thaddaeus, or Lebbaeus. Judas Thaddaeus became known as Jude after early translators of the New Testament from Greek into English sought to distinguish him from Judas Iscariot and subsequently abbreviated his forename. Most versions of the New Testament in languages other than English and French, refer to Judas and Jude by the same name. (Luke 6:16 KJV)

Thaddaeus, was sometimes referred to as the brother of Jesus. Jesus had four half brothers and at least two half sisters; maybe three. (Matthew 13:55-56; Mark 6:3 KJV)

According to tradition, Apostle St. Jude suffered martyrdom about 65 A.D in Beirut, in the Roman province of Syria, together with the apostle Simon the Zealot, with whom he is usually connected. The axe that he is often shown holding in pictures symbolizes the way in which he was killed. Their acts and martyrdom were recorded in an Acts of Simon and Jude that was among the collection of passions and legends traditionally associated with the legendary Abdias, bishop of Babylon, and said to have been translated into Latin by his disciple, Tropaeus Africanus, according to the Golden Legend account of the saints.

Sometime after his death, Saint Jude's body was brought from Beirut to Rome and placed in a crypt in St. Peter's Basilica which was visited by many devotees. His bones are allegedly in the left transept of St. Peter's Basilica under the main altar of

St. Joseph in one tomb with the remains of the apostle Simon the Zealot. However, according to another popular tradition, the remains of St. Jude have been removed and are preserved in a desolate stronghold in the Pamir Mountains or the Pamirs. The Pamirs, are a mountain range in Central Asia at the junction of the Himalayas with the Tian Shan, Karakoram, Junlun, Hindu Kush and Hindu Raj ranges. They are among the worlds's highest mountains.

THOMAS

Thomas, also called Didymus, being Greek for twin, was a skeptic and had a gloomy outlook on life. Thomas questioned Jesus on many things (John 14:5: 20:25-28. KJV) Sounds like many of the church folks and politicians.

Slow to believe and at one time known as "doubting Thomas", due to his unbelief concerning the resurrection of Jesus,(John 11:16 KJV) Thomas was still willing to die for him (John 11:16 KJV).

At the Last Supper, when Jesus assumed that the disciples knew the way to the Father's house, Thomas was honest and forthright enough to confess openly his ignorance. "Lord, we do not know where you are going; how can we know the way?" (John 14:5 KJV)

Thomas had been fishing on the Sea of Galilee with six other disciples, having caught nothing, when Jesus appeared to them the third time after his resurrection (John:21:1-14 KJV). Being directed, by the Lord, to cast their net on the right side of the boat, they brought in a net full of fish an then had breakfast to-gather.

Thomas is remembered for his incredulity when the other Apostles announced Christ's Resurrection to him: "Except I shall see in his hands the print of the nails, and put my finger into the place of the nails, and put my hand into his side, I will not believe. (John 20:25 KJV)

Being a loyal follower of Jesus after the ascension, it is possible Thomas was one of the ones who had gathered in a prayer meeting with eleven, some women, Mary the mother of Jesus and his brethren praying for the release of Peter from jail (Acts 1:12-14 KJV). Thomas could have been one of the main ones who did not believe Peter had been released from jail when Peter showed up at the house where the prayer meeting was on going (Acts 12:12-17 KJV).

There are questionable traditions concerning the missionary activities of Thomas. After the resurrection of Jesus, Thomas went to Babylon and is believed that he established the first Christian church there. He also went to Persia and from there he went to India, preaching the gospel. Thomas is believed to have been a fearless evangelist, a great builder of churches, and successful in having many converts. It is believed that he preached in China and arrived in India no later than 49 A.D. According to Origen, cited by Eusebius, Hist. III.I, Thomas worked in Parthia. He supposedly experienced many trials in India.

According to Clement of Alexandria, Stromateis, Bk 4, Thomas died a natural death and was buried by his converts.

Although one tradition states that while Thomas was in India, he suffered martyrdom and was killed with a lance and buried in Mylapore, India, which is now a suburb of Madras. It is believed he died on the 21st of December. Another tradition states that his remains were brought to Edessa in Mesopotamia, and from there to Ortona in Italy during the Crusades.

His alleged remains were exhibited as late as the 16th century.

JUDAS

J udas is certainly the most enigmatic disciple in the gospel story. The meaning of his name or designation, his background, character, motive in betraying Jesus and the manner of his death are riddles quite insolvable.

The most diverse explanations have been offered for the name Iscariot: "man from Kerioth"; "the assassin; "man of Issachar"; "man from Sychar" meaning a Samaritan, " "man from Jericho"; "carrier of the leather bag", (scortea); "false one, liar, hypocrite". By far the commonest interpretation is the first; "man from Kerioth."

If the name, in spite of difficulties, is taken to mean "man from Kerioth", it may be held that this disciple was thus designated because he was the only Judean among the twelve.

Jesus may have chosen Judas because he saw possibilities of novility and great usefulness in him. One scholar has suggested that he was the brother of Mary, Martha, and Lazarus, whose complaint was the waste of ointment and was motivated by a purely selfish interest (John 12:4-6 KJV). Is it possible this may have caused Judas to hold some ill will, in his heart, toward Jesus?

The name Judas is always placed last as a disciple (Matthew 10:2-4; Mark 3:16-19; Luke 6:14-16 KJV), but he was a very important member of the twelve. The listing as being last undoubtedly is because of the betrayal, but the fact that Judas was treasurer of the group (John 12:6; 13:29 KJV) and being with Jesus at the Last Supper, contradicts the lowly listing (John 13:21-26 KJV). Eastern church tradition held that his name once stood higher in the apostolic list; third or sixth.

The motives behind Judas betrayal of Jesus are unascertainable. So obscure or so obviously slanted are the accounts of Judas' treachery and death, that some scholars have doubted the historicity of the betrayal. However, the primitive church would hardly have invented an episode so infamous and derogatory to one of the disciples.

With the passing of time, the name Judas became more and more blackened with the fourth Gospel practically identifying him with satan, and the Antichrist (John 6:70; 17:12 KJV), but the crescendo in hostility should not undermine belief in the historicity of the event itself.

Did the enthusiasm of Judas for Jesus gradually cool? Was he disappointed because Jesus failed to strike decisively at his enemies and the enemies of the nation-in-fact, even running away from them on one occasion? Did Judas stumble over Jesus indifference to many points of the law and perhaps resent his association with the wrong people; tax collectors and sinners? Was the supreme disappointment the failure of Jesus to manifest his power in the Holy city, after he had doggedly journeyed there for a showdown appearance? At the last, did Judas sincerely believe Jesus a false messiah, a deceiver of the people, who according to the law should be done away with (Deut. 13:1-11 KJV)? The late Dr. Albert Schweitzer believed that Jesus was a prophet who failed.

Some theologians argue that Judas, by the betrayal, was attempting to force Jesus into a display of power so that the religious and political authorities would be convinced of his messiahship. If he really was the Messiah, could he not call on a legion of angels to deliver him? Thus all doubt would be cleared away and the nation would be won to him. Others argue Judas is the antichrist and was predestined to betray Jesus and he could not do anything about it. It is my belief that Judas is not the antichrist. Judas killed himself, but the antichrist will be put to death by Christ (Daniel 7:11; 11:45; 2 Thessalonians 2:8; Revelations 19:20 KJV). The antichrist or King of the north, Syria, will make his capital the Jewish temple in Jerusalem between the Dead Sea and the Mediterranean Sea in the mountain, Mount Moriah, but will be put to death at Armageddon (Daniel 11:45; 7:11, 26,27; 8:25; 9:27; 2 Thessalonians 2:8; Revelations 19:20 KJV). The antichrist will be put to death in the lake of fire (Daniel 7:11; Isaiah 11:4; Revelations 19:20; 20:10 KJV).

Exactly what information Judas delivered to the religious authorities for his thirty pieces of silver is unclear. Was it that

Jesus had accepted anointing at Bethany and thus openly claimed messiahship (Mark 13:3-11 KJV)? Or was it simply that Judas provided them the place of Jesus' nocturnal retreat so that he could be apprehended quietly without exciting his many sympathizers and supporters (MARK 14:1-2 KJV)? The latter supposition better accords with the gospel representation.

There are those who question if Judas partook of the feet washing and Last Supper and is still debated today. According to the scriptures, there is no question of his involvement when Jesus said,(Matthew 26:20, Mark 14:20, Luke 22:14-23, John 13:18-26 KJV) "the hand of him that betrayeth me is with me on the table" (Matthew 26:20-25; Mark 14:20; Luke 22:14-23; John 13:18, 26 KJV). By Jesus using the word betrayeth, would lead one to believe Judas had already betrayed Jesus. Jesus knew who he had chosen as disciples, but so that the scriptures could be fulfilled, the one that eateth bread with him is the one that will betray him. "He it is, to whom I shall give a sop, when I have dipped it".(John 13:18, John 13:26 KJV) And when he had dipped the sop, he gave it to Judas Iscariot, the son of Simon (John 13:18, 26; 13:26 KJV).

The participation of Judas in the covenant fellowship would raise theological problems. In view of the tendency in the tradition concerning Judas to reduce him to the status of a devil, Luke's more theologically difficult and less tendentious account of the Supper, may contain historic fact. If Judas participated in this holy sacrament, his subsequent deed appears the more reprehensible.

The demise of Judas is shrouded in the same obscurity as the events leading up to it. According to Mark and Luke, Judas offered to betray Jesus to the chief priests and would receive thirty pieces of silver, thus becoming the first government paid informant or "snitch".

God predicted this betrayal in Zech. 11:12-13 and His prediction was fulfilled (Matthew 27:3 KJV).

Matthew pictures Judas as repenting, feeling remorse for what he had done, but not asking God to forgive him, and offered to return the money to the priests (Matthew 27:3 KJV), but refusing to accept the coins, Judas threw down the money, in the temple, and departed and went and hanged himself (Matthew 27:4-5 KJV). Had Judas really repented, asking forgiveness of God, regardless of whether the money was accepted by the chief priests, he would not have killed himself.

Repentance is found in the King James Bible more than 100 times from Gen. 6 to Rev. 16.

The priests, unwilling to place "blood money" in the temple treasure, purchased with it a potter's field, which became known as the "field of blood". This plot of ground, is assumed to be located in the Kidron, tyropoeon and Hinnom valleys. Another belief is this field is known as Aceldama, and is located near the Greek orthodox church and convent of Saint oniprius, which is southeast of Jerusalem. This according to writer Borchard.

A widely divergent story is told alluding to which Judas himself buys the field and through a headlong fall, or swelling up, is disembowled (Acts 1:18-19 KJV) The writer Lightfoot describes the devil taking Judas up in the air and dashed his body on the ground after strangling him. Another belief is Judas hung himself over a cliff and the tree branch that he had tied the rope or his girdle to, and placed around his neck, broke thus flinging him over the cliff and landed on the jagged rocks below. Another theory is after hanging from the branch for several days, his body began to swell or distend, meaning to become bloated and turgid from internal pressure or to expand, stretch out or blow up, thus causing the rope to break. Dr. Luke, being a man of medicine, understood all the entrails or internal organs of the middle and lower ventricle thus possible explaining his description (Acts 1:18 KJV). In the description of Lightfoot, it is possible that the devil had been in Judas for three days prior to him hanging himself. This is based on the assumption that it had been three days from the time Judas betrayed Jesus until he actually hung himself. If this be true, the devil had full control and possession of Judas. In (Luke 9:42 KJV), the devil threw him down and tore him apart. With the devil in control of one's life, anything is possible.

The manner in which Judas died was much commented on by early Christian preachers and writers and all sorts of gruesome details were introduced to make the death more horrible.

Both biblical and post biblical accounts of the death of Judas appear to have been influenced by Old Testament and apocryphal stories of the demise of evil men, the LXX account of the death of Ahithophel, (2 Samuel 17:23 KJV); Antiochus Epiphanes II Macc. 9-7-18, Nadan, story of Ahikar, or at least by a loose tradition concerning the way traitors and villains should die. The two New Testament accounts agree only that Judas died violently as a consequence of his act and that a plot of ground in Jerusalem was purchased (Matthew 27:8 KJV), with the thirty pieces of silver; $19.20 or about 113 days wages of common laborer at .17 cents a day. A slave could also be purchased for this price (Exodus 21:32 KJV). An inmate in a federal prison camp only makes about $1.00 a day. Maybe the powers that be has read Exodus!!!!!!!!!!!!!!!!

BETRAYAL OF JESUS FORETOLD

S everal passages in the Bible tell us Jesus knew He would be betrayed. Jesus knew from the beginning who would betray him (John 6:64 KJV), however, only at the Last Supper is it revealed who that person was. Only in (Matthew 20:19 and 26:2 KJV) does it tell us that Jesus predicted He would die by crucifixion. Mark, Luke and John only tell us Jesus would be killed. The word crucifixion is used more than forty times in the N.T. and means to impale on a cross. The Romans and Greeks copied this form of punishment from the Phoenicians and inflicted it on what they considered the worst criminals and slaves. This practice was continued until Constantine in the 4th century.

Having charged his disciples that they should tell no one that He was Jesus the Christ (Matthew 16:20; Mark 9:30 KJV), He began to show them how He must go to Jerusalem and suffer many things of the church folks and politicians. He would eventually suffer death, but on the third day, He would be raised from the dead (Mt. 16:21; Mark 9:31-32; Luke 9:22 KJV).

There are those who have questioned that Jesus did not stay in the grave three full days; that he arose on the third day. The scriptures tell us that Jesus said, "For as Jonas was three days and three nights in the belly of the whale (Jonah 1:17 KJV), so shall the Son of man be three days and three nights in the heart of the earth (Matthew 12:40 KJV). If this be true, then Jesus would not have come out of the grave until the fourth day. Mark 8:31 also says that Jesus would be killed and rise after three days. All the other scriptures indicate Jesus would rise on the third day (Matthew 16:21; 17:23; 20:19; Mark 9:31; 10:34; Luke 9:22; 18:33; 24:7; Acts 10:40; 1 Corinthians 15:4 KJV). The Hebrew idiom three days can be used for any part of three days, but things change when you add the word nights. This can only mean three full days to have three full nights.

When Jesus, Peter, James and his brother John were come to the multitude, there came a man to Jesus informing him that the disciples had not been able to cast the devil out of his lunatick son and ask Jesus to have mercy on him. Having called the disciples a faithless and perverse generation,(Matthew 17:1 KJV) Jesus proceeded to rebuke the devil; and he departed out of the child (Matthew 17:1 KJV).

The disciples approached Jesus, away from the multitude, and wanted to know why they had been unable to perform the miracle. Jesus said, "Because of your unbelief." Jesus went on to tell them if they had the faith as a grain of mustard seed, they could not only move a mountain, but nothing would be impossible unto them; But they could only do it by prayer and fasting. While still in Galilee, Jesus informed them, "The Son of Man shall be betrayed in the hands of men"(Matthew 17:13-23 KJV). It is possible that this is where Jesus had to rebuke Peter and tell him, "Get the behind me Satan: for thou savourest not the things that be of God, but the things that be of men" (Mark 8:32-33 KJV).

Dr. Luke records this meeting a little different concerning the instructions that Jesus gave to Peter. In paraphrasing Dr. Luke, Jesus said to Peter,James and John, "Get it thru your thick skull and let it sink down into your ears: the Son of man shall be delivered into the hands of men." (Luke 9:44-45 KJV) The disciples still did not understand what he was telling them and they were afraid to ask (Luke 9:44-45 KJV).

On one of his many journeys to Jerusalem, Jesus informed all the disciples that, "The Son of man shall be betrayed unto the politicians and church folks, and will be abused, then killed by the Gentiles" (Matthew20:17-19; Mark 110-32; Luke 18:31-33 KJV).

Two days before the Passover and being the end of the ministry of Jesus, He told the disciples,(Matthew 26:1-2 KJV) "The Son of man is betrayed"(Matthew 26:1-2 KJV). This is the only time that Jesus spoke of His betrayal having already taken place.

On the first day of the feast, this being our Tuesday sunset to Wednesday sunset, the disciples came to Jesus asking Him at what place did he want them to have the Passover. Jesus asked them to go into the city and inform this certain man that Jesus' time was at hand and his house would be used for the Passover (Matthew 26:17-18 KJV).

Have your ever wondered who the owner of this house was and Jesus chose this certain man. Could it have been a relative or just a close personal friend? When politicians travel throughout the world, sometimes, they will spend the night with a close personal friend or a supporter instead of spending the night in a motel. This could have been for security reasons why Jesus chose this man and his house.

The final time Jesus forewarned the disciples of His betrayal and death, was the night of the Passover when the disciples joined Him for His last supper.

Prior to partaking of the last supper, Jesus stood up, laid aside His garments, took a towel and girded himself. He proceeded to pour water into a basin and began to wash the disciples feet. When he had finished, using the towel wrapped around Him, He dried their feet.

Peter at first, refused to permit Jesus to wash his feet, but after Jesus said, "If I wash the not, thou hast no part with me."(John 13:8 KJV) Peter immediately changed his mind. Then Jesus said, "He that is washed needeth not save to wash his feet, but is clean every whit: and ye are clean, but not all. Jesus knew who should betray Him; therefore saying, "Ye are not all clean." (John 13: 9-11 KJV).

Some scholars have different opinions on whether Judas

permitted Jesus to wash his feet. No where does the scriptures say He washed all the disciples feet except Judas. After Jesus poured the water in the basin, (John 13:5 KJV)He began to wash the disciples feet (John 13:5 KJV). When the even was come, Jesus sat down with the twelve and the supper followed the foot washing (Matthew 26:20; Matthew 26:21 KJV).

Prior to the supper beginning, and after the washing of the feet, and Jesus having dressed, He sat down and began talking to them. "Know ye what I have done to you?"(John 13:12 KJV) Jesus went on to admonish the disciples to wash each others feet as He had washed theirs. "For I have given you an example that ye should do as I have done you." (John 13:15 KJV)

Having heard this, the disciples were prepared to began the meal when Jesus said, "I know whom I have chosen, but the scriptures have to be fulfilled. He that eats bread with me, hath lifted up his heel against me (Jn. 13:18). As Jesus continued to talk and testify, He was troubled in spirit and said,(John 13:21) "Verily, Verily, I say unto, that one of you shall betray me" (John 13:21 KJV).

The disciples were exceeding sorrowful and each one began asking Jesus which disciple was he referring to? This indicates the other disciples still was not aware of what Judas had done or would do (Matthew 26:22 KJV).

It is my opinion that John is the disciple, lying on Jesus' breast asked, "Lord who is it?" (John 13:23; John 19:25-27; John 20:2; John 21:7 KJV) Each of these scriptures refer to that disciple that Jesus loved. It was no secret that Jesus and John were very close.

In response to John's question, Jesus responded saying,(Matthew 26:20-24, Mark 14:17-21,; Luke 22:21-23 KJV) "he that dippeth his hand with me in the dish, the same shall betray me." Jesus continued,(Matthew 26:20-24; Luke 22:21-23; Mark 14:17-21;Luke 22:21-23 KJV) "The Son of man goeth as it is written of him: but woe unto that man by whom the Son of man is betrayed: it would have been good for that man if he had not been born. (Matthew 26:20-24; Mark 14:17-21; Luke 22:21-23 KJV).

Dr. Luke records the event a little different saying that Jesus responded to John, still not calling the name of Judas, "He it is, to whom I shall give a sop, when I have dipped it (John 13:26 KJV). Only in (John 13:26, 27, 30 KJV) does the scriptures refer to sop. The Greek word for sop, (psomion), means a morsel. This was a portion of the paschal supper, collected in the fingers and dipped in the sauce, and handed to the guests. This was considered a mark of honor for the guest who received it. It is apparent that Judas had not responded as Jesus appealed to his conscience, so now it is probable that Jesus was appealing to his heart.

Judas then ask Jesus, (Matthew 26 :25 KJV)"Master, is it I?" Jesus responded, (Matthew 26:25 KJV) "Thou hast said" (Matthew 26:25 KJV). When Jesus dipped the sop, He gave it to Judas Iscariot, son of Simon. After the sop, Satan entered into

Judas. Then said Jesus, (John 13:27 KJV)"That thou doest, do quickly"(John. 13:27 KJV). Judas could have still backed away from betraying Jesus and remained faithful, but apparently his heart was hardened.

The disciples still did not understand what Jesus was talking about, and why he said this to Judas. They imagined Jesus was referring to Judas, since he was the treasurer, telling him to pay for the cost of the feast (John 13:28-29 KJV).

Upon receiving the sop, Judas went immediately out; this already being Tuesday night (John 13:30 KJV). As Judas left the room, Jesus said, (John 13:31 KJV)"Now is the Son of man glorified, and God is glorified in Him." Jesus was glorified that He had been appointed to be the Savior of the world, and God was glorified in Jesus (John 13:31 KJV).

Have you wondered why Judas asked Jesus, "Master is it I?"(Matthew 26:25 KJV) Not one time had Jesus called Judas by name as the one who would betray Him. Is it possible that Judas was testing Jesus to see if He really knew? Was it possible that Judas was having second thoughts about his plan?

Even though Jesus knew that Judas would betray Him, He still shared His meal with him and wanted to be his friend. The hand of Jesus is still extended to anyone who believes and wants to be saved.

THE ARREST AND TRIAL OF JESUS

After Judas departed the room where the Last Supper was being held, Jesus continued sharing with the eleven still in the room. He was telling them about Him going to leave them and about the future and the way they should live. In response to his remark, (John 14:36 KJV)"Where I go, you cannot follow me now; but you shall follow Me afterwards," Peter said unto Him, Lord, why cannot I follow You now?" (John 14:37 KJV) Peter continues, "I will lay down my life for Your sake." Jesus responded, (John 10:18 KJV)"Will you lay down your life for My sake?" "Verily, verily, I say unto you, the rooster will not crow, till you have denied Me thrice."(John 10:18 KJV)

When Jesus had spoken these words, He left the building with His disciples and went across the Kidron Valley, where there was a garden, which he and his disciples entered (John 18:1 KJV). The Kidron Valley is actually a dry waterbed with water only during rainy season, so crossing it in April would have not involved getting wet. This site is still identifiable.

The garden is the "Garden of Gethsemane." It is located

somewhere on the lower slopes of the Mount of Olives, and is very likely where arrest of Jesus took place. Now Judas also knew the place, for Jesus often met there with the disciples. (John 18:2-3 KJV). No question Judas was very familiar with this location and knew this would be a very good place to find Jesus.

Judas having procured a band of soldiers and some officers from the chief priests and the Pharisees, went there with the lanterns, torches and weapons. Not only did Judas betray Jesus, but assembled the soldiers and officers who went with him. (John 18:3-5 KJV)

The officers from the Chief Priest and Pharisees making the arrest of Jesus, were probably the temple guards who had authority under the Jewish leaders to make arrests. The Roman soldiers did not arrest Jesus, they simply accompanied the temple guard for added security.

Upon arrival at the place where Jesus was, Jesus came forward and said to them, "Whom do you seek?" They responded "Jesus of Nazareth." Jesus said unto them, "I am He." Judas, who had betrayed Jesus with a kiss, was standing with them. (John 18:4-5 KJV)

When Jesus said to them, "I am He", they drew back and fell to the ground. Jesus asked them again, "Whom do you seek?" And they responded, "Jesus of Nazareth." Jesus answered again, "I told you that I am he. So, if you seek me, let these men go." (John 18: 6-8 KJV)

Then Simon Peter, having a sword, drew it and struck the high priest's servant Malchus, cutting off his right ear. Jesus said to Peter, put your sword into its sheath; shall I not drink the cup that the Father has given me?" Jesus touched Malchus ear and healed it. (John 18: 10-11 KJV) (Luke 22:51 KJV)

At this time, Jesus was arrested and bound like a common criminal and took him to Annas for questioning. The scribes and the elders were all there. They sought false witnesses against Him, wanting to put Him to death. The men that held Jesus, mocked him and smote him. They even blindfolded Jesus and struck him on the face and asked him to prophesy who had struck him. No witnesses cold be found. (Luke 22:63-65 KJV)

The night of the arrest of Jesus, He was brought before Annas, Caiaphas, and an assembly of religious leaders called the Sanhedrin (John 18:19-24; Matthew 26:27KJV). After this, He was taken before Pilate, the Roman Governor (John 18:23 KJV), sent off to in Herod (Luke 23:7, and returned to Pilate (Luke 23:11-12 KJV), who finally sentenced Him to death.

There were six parts of Jesus' trial: three stages in a religious court and three stages before a Roman court. Jesus was tried before Annas, the former high priest: Caiaphas, the current high priest: and the Sanhedrin. He was charged in these "ecclesiastical" trials with blasphemy, claiming to be the Son of God. (John 18:25 KJV)

Annas, was the father-in-law of Caiaphas who was high

priest that year. This position was the most powerful office in Jewish Palestine, but was removed by the Roman government later. According to Jewish Law, no single individual could act as judge in a capital case, but this did not stop Aannas from privately interrogating Jesus. Caiaphas had advised the Jews that it would be expedient that one man should die for the people. (John 18:13 KJV)

Standing before Annas, he asked Jesus about his disciples and his doctrine. Jesus responded that(John 18:20) "He had spoke openly in the world; having taught in the synagogue and in the temple, whither the Jews always resort; and in secret have I said nothing." Why ask me what I have said unto them. Ask them. They know what . (John 18:20 KJV)

I have said.(John 18:20 KJV) "At this time, one of the officers struck Jesus with the palm of his hand ordering him to answer the high priest. Jesus responded, "If I have spoken evil, bear witness of the evil, bear witness of the evil; but if well, why smitest thou me?" (JOHN 18:23 KJV)

At some point, a fire was built in the hall and they sat down together. Peter sat down with them, but not close by. One certain maiden in the crowd, spotted Peter and cried out, this man was with Jesus also. Peter responded by saying, "Woman, I know Him not." This was the first denial by Peter. (Luke 22:59 KJV)

A little while later, another one in the crowd spotted Peter and said, "You are also of them." Peter responded, "Man, I am not." This was the second denial. (Luke 22:59-60-61 KJV)

After about an hour, Peter was spotted again and the person said, "Of a truth, this fellow also was with him: for he is a Gallilian." Peter responded, "Man, I know not what you say." This was the third denial. Immediately, while he yet spoke, the rooster crowed. Jesus turned, looked upon Peter. Peter remembered what Jesus had predicted and he went out and wept bitterly (Luke 22:62 KJV).

Having questioned Jesus at length, Annas had Jesus bound and sent to Caiphas for disposition of this case. Reminds me of some of the judges of today. If something comes before them they don't want to handle, they will bring in another judge. (John 18:24 KJV)

After appearing before Caiphas, Jesus had to appear before four more courts before actually being sentenced to death by Pilate (Luke 23:11-12 KJV).

The trials before Jewish authorities, the religious trials, showed the degree to which the Jewish leaders hated Him because they carelessly disregarded many of their own laws. There were several illegalities involved in these trials from the perspective of Jewish law: (1) No trial was to be held during feast time. (2) Each member of the court was to vote individually to convict or acquit, but Jesus was convicted by acclamation. (3) If the death penalty was given, a night must pass before the sentence was carried out; however, only a few hours passed before Jesus was placed on the Cross. (4) The Jews had no authority to execute anyone. (5) No trial was to be held at night, but this trial was held before dawn. (6) The accused was to be given counsel or representation, but Jesus had none. (7) The accused was not to be asked self-incriminating questions, but Jesus was asked if He was the Christ.

The trials before the Roman authorities started with Pilate (John 18:23 KJV) after Jesus was beaten. The charges brought against Him were very different from the charges in His religious trials. He was charged with inciting people to riot, forbidding the people to pay their taxes, and claiming to be King. Pilate found no reason to kill Jesus so he sent Him to Herod (Luke 23:7 KJV). Herod had Jesus ridiculed but, wanting to avoid the political liability, sent Jesus back to Pilate (Luke 23:11-12 KJV). This was the last trial as Pilate tried to appease the animosity of the Jews by having Jesus scourged. The Roman scourge was a terrible whipping designed to remove the flesh from the back of the one being punished. In a final effort to have Jesus released, Pilate offered the prisoner Barabbas to be crucified and Jesus released, but no avail. The crowds called for Barabbas to be released and Jesus to be crucified. Plate granted their demand and surrendered Jesus to their will (Luke 23:21 KJV). The trials of Jesus represent the ultimate mockery of justice. Jesus, the most innocent man in the history of the world, was found guilty of crimes and sentenced to death by crucifixion.

Even though He is Jesus, while on earth, He was human so like thousands of people in the United States, by his being

charged, arrested, found guilty and sentenced to die, Jesus became a convicted felon and received the death penalty.

JUDAS REPLACED

Following the Ascension, the disciples returned to Jerusalem from the Mount of Olive, about a day's journey, went into an upper room where abode the eleven disciples (Acts 1:12-13 KJV).

In the upper room with the disciples, were women, Mary the mother of Jesus and his brethren (Acts 1:14 KJV). The women who were in the upper room were the ones that had followed Jesus from Galilee (Matthew 27:55-56 KJV). Peter informed the disciples that there were a total of one hundred twenty present (Acts 1:15 KJV). Under the Jewish law, 120 were the number of men required to form a council in a city.

Having called the meeting to order, the first order of business of the church (Acts 1:15-20 KJV), was to provide qualifications for candidates that wanted to be considered to replace Judas (Acts 1:21-22 KJV). The ones who were permitted to nominate, appointed two for consideration. Joseph, called Barsabas, referred to as Justus Barsabas (Acts 4:36 KJV), and surnamed Justus and Matthias (Acts 1:23KJV). Justus, being interpreted the son of encouragement, was a Levite and of the country of cyprus (Acts 4:36 KJV). Justus had a piece of property he sold and gave a certain portion to the Apostles (Acts 4:37 KJV). Is it possible that Justus was trying to buy a spot on the council? If this was his motive, it did not work.

Nomination being completed, they prayed, asking God for wisdom in making their selection (Acts 1:24 KJV). Once the lots were given forth, the lot fell on Matthias and he was numbered with the eleven (Acts 1:26 KJV).

Had this event taken place today, an election would have taken place using sophisticated voting equipment. However, in the days of the disciples, the common way was to inscribe the names on parchment, wood or stone, placing them in a urn and after prayer, someone would reach their hand in and withdraw one of the lots (Lev. 16:8-9 KJV); (Joshua 14:2 KJV).

There has been much discussion through the years why Paul was not chosen as the replacement of Judas. There is no question he would have been an excellent choice. However, the qualifications that were set precluded Paul from being a candidate. Candidates must have "accompanied" Jesus and the disciples from the days when John baptized to the time of the ascension of Jesus, and that he also had to be a witness to the resurrection of Jesus (Acts 1:2-22 KJV).

Apostle Matthias was born at Bethlehem of the Tribe of Judah. From his early childhood, he studied the Law of God under the guidance of St. Simeon the God-receiver.

When Jesus revealed himself to the world, St. Matthias

believed in him as the Messiah, followed constantly after him and was numbered among the Seventy Apostles, whom the lord "sent them two by two before His face" (Luke 10:1 KJV).

After the Descent of the Holy Spirit, the Apostle Matthias preached the Gospel at Jerusalem and in Judea together with the other Apostles (Acts 6:2, 8:14 KJV). From Jerusalem he went with the Apostles Peter and Andrew to Syrian Antioch, and was in the Cappadocian city of Tianum and Sinope. Here, he was locked into prison, from which he was miraculously freed by St. Andrew the First-Called.

Having been released from prison, Apostle Matthias preached in numerous places and was frequently subjected to deadly peril, but the Lord preserved him to preach the Gospel.

On another occasion while in prison, pagans forced him to drink a poison potion. He not only remained unharmed, but also healed other prisoners who had been blinded by the potion. When St. Matthias was released, the pagans searched for him in vain, for he had become invisible to them. Another time, when the pagans had become enraged intending to kill the Apostle, the earth opened up and engulfed them.

The Apostle Matthias returned to Judea and continued preaching and working great miracles in the name of Jesus and was successful in converting many to faith in Christ. (Acts 1:12 KJV)

The Jewish High Priest Ananias hated Jesus and earlier had commanded the Apostle James, brother of Jesus, to be flung down from the heights of the Temple and now he ordered Matthias be arrested and brought before the Sanhedrin at Jerusalem. There, the impious Ananias uttered a speech in which he blasphemously slandered the Lord. Using the prophecies of the Old Testament, Apostle Matthias demonstrated that Jesus Christ is the True God, the promised Messiah, the Son of God, Consubstantial and Coeternal with God the Father. After these words, the Matthias was sentenced to death by the Sanhedrin and was stoned. (Acts 7:11 KJV)

After Matthias was dead, the Jews, to hide their malefaction, cut off his head as an enemy of Caesar. However, according to several historians, the Apostle Matthais was crucified, and died at Colchis.

Apostle Matthias received the martyr's crown of glory in the year 63.

Facts about Judas

A Disciple (Matthew 10: Mark 3:13-19 KJV)

Ordained Preacher (Mark 4:14 KJV)

Possessed power to heal (Mark 3:13-15 KJV)

Endued with power and the Spirit speaking through them (Matthew 10:1-20 KJV)

Successful preacher and healer (Mark 6:7-13; Luke 9:6-10 KJV)

Water baptizer (John 4:1-2 KJV)

Possessed eternal life at one time (John 17:2 KJV)

Once saved with name in Book of Life (Pslams 69:25-28; Luke 10:20; Mark 6:13; Acts 1:20 KJV)

Promise of an eternal kingship (Matthew 19:28 KJV)

First treasurer of the church (Jn. 12:4:-6; 13:29)

Well known to Jesus (Psalms 41:9 KJV) Hebrew for familiar means shalom, safe, favored, perfect, friend

A confident of Jesus (Psalms 41:9 KJV), Having known what is in men (John 2:25 KJV), Jesus knew that Judas, being saved and a disciple could be trusted; until he backslid.

Consummated betrayal of Jesus with a kiss (Matthew 26:48-49 KJV)

Woe unto him, or lost (Mark 14:21 KJV)

Backslid meaning fell from grace under NT, because of transgression (Acts 1:20-25 KJV) Judas went to place prepared for all unrepentant backsliders (Psalms 9:17; Matthew 25:41; 26:24; Revelations 21:8 KJV)

CURSES ON JUDAS AND PRIESTS

*T*he Betrayer and crucifer of Jesus
Predicted in Psalms 69:22-28KJV - Fulfilled in Acts 1:20

Their table shall become a snare.

Their benefits shall become a trap

Eyes darkened

Be made blind

Continuous shaking of the loins

Wrath poured upon them

Habitations be desolate

Tents remain empty

Iniquity added to iniquity

No righteousness known

Name blotted out of Book of Life

Name not written with righteous

COMPARISONS OF JUDAS

*A*hithophel as traitors
*Palms. 55:12-14 KJV - Fulfilled John 13:18-19 KJV; Acts
1:1 KJV*

Friends of masters - vs 12, 13

Betrayed and reproached their former friend

Lovers of their master

Magnified themselves against their best friend

Untrustworthy

Equals in trust

Guides - Counselors

Known by their master

Enjoyed sweet fellowship with their master

Attended and worshipped together in the same place of worship

Betrayal of the messiah predicted (Psalms 41:9 KJV) Fulfilled (John. 13:1 KJV)

Yea, mine own familiar friend, in whom I trusted, which did eat of my bread, hath lifted up his heel against me.

DID JUDAS BACKSLIDE
AND GO TO HELL?

A
ll my life I have heard, once you are saved, no matter what you do from then on, you will remain saved. Sort of like once you are born, you will always be the child of your parents; regardless of whether you are bad or good. The latter part I believe, but that is dealing with physical and not spiritual. What does the King James Bible tell us? If you do not believe the word of God, then there is no need in continuing to read.

Through out the Bible, there are several documented cases of angels, demons, men, as well as others who have backslid. They once were saved, but turned away from God and were lost.

The devil, Lucifer, walked with God at one time, and was perfect and a sinless angel, but he sinned(Ezek. 28:11-19 KJV). God got a belly full of him and threw him out of heaven (Isaiah 14:12-15; Luke 10:18 KJV) because of his lies, sinfulness and lustfulness, (John 8:44 KJV), and was sent to hell (Matthew

25:41; Revelations 20:1-10 KJV).

What about the angels that chose sides with the devil (Rev. 12:4), thus choosing hell over heaven? (Isaiah 24:21; Matthew 25:41) KJV. Lucifer was already a fallen creature when he came to the Garden of Eden (Genesis 2:2 KJV). The great dragon is used as a symbol of Satan (Job 42; Psalms 91:13; Isaiah 27:1; Revelations 12:3-17; 13:2-4; 16:13; 20:2 KJV).

Many of the angels were thrown out of heaven (2 Peter 2:4 KJV) because of fornication (Genesis 6:4; Jude 6:7 KJV). Angels are sons of God (Genesis 6:1-4; Job 1:6; 2:1; 38:4-7 KJV), and they were cast forever into hell for their sins. If this be true, it is apparent that no one has an unforfeitable guarantee of Heaven.

Let's look at the demons who were created in God's grace and favor and who were sinless. Not only did they sin and doomed to hell, they are in the Abys, bottomless pit, waiting to be released, to fulfill the vision of Revelation 9.

God created Adam and Eve in His grace and favor (Genesis 1:26-31 KJV), but they fell from grace because of sin and lost eternal life (Genesis 2:17; 3:1-19; Romans 5:12-21; 2 Corinthians 11:3 KJV). At the age of 810, Adam was still a sinner (Genesis 6:3 KJV) and was given 120 more years to live. Although, a son of God, there is no indication Adam ever repented (Genesis 6:7 KJV). ONCE AGAIN, SON-SHIP IS NOT A GUARANTEE OF ETERNAL LIFE!

Many disciples of Jesus left Him and His grace and followed Him no more (John 6:66 KJV). Even though they believed at one time (Luke 8:13 KJV), they were drawn back to perdition (Hebrews 10:26-39 KJV). These disciples were not the chosen twelve. Jesus said unto them, "Will ye also go away?" (John 6:67 KJV).

Saul, a great leader, was given a new heart and the spirit of God came upon him (1 Samuel 10:9-10 KJV). Saul backslid and committed suicide. (1 Samuel 16:14; 1 Samuel 31:4-6 KJV).

Demas, a preacher backslid (2 Timothy 4:10 KJV), because he loved the world. Anyone who loves the world, cannot have the love of God in him (1 John 2:15-17 KJV). If Demus did not repent, and I find no indication tht he did, then Demus could not have had the love of God in him. Without the love of God, there is no way Demus could have been saved (John 13:35; 14:15-23; 15:9-12; 1 Corinthians 16:22. KJV)

Some others who backslid were many young widows (1 Timothy 5:11-15 KJV), The Galatians (Galations 1:6; 4:8-9; Jude 4:1 KJV), and Hymenaeus and Alexander (1 Timothy 1:19:-20 KJV). To accept Jesus and confess Him for only a short time, and turn back, gives fall from grace (John 1:12; 1 John 5:1 KJV). Jesus gave His life so that anyone who meets all the conditions, can have eternal life. However, they must continue to honor the conditions. It is a free choice whether a person accepts eternal life or not (John 3:16; Timothy 2:4; 2 Peter 3:9; Revelations 22:17 KJV).

There will be many of my personal friends, as well as others, who will become upset and disagree with the following, but based on my interpretation of the word of God, and until I am shown different, I am of the opinion Judas backslid, committed suicide and was lost (Psalms 69:22-28; Matthew 26:24; Mark 14:21; Luke 22:22; John 17:12; Acts 1:16-25 KJV). Had Judas not been saved, would Jesus have chosen him as one of the twelve? Would Jesus call an unsaved person or the devil, "my own familiar friends (Psalms 41:9 KJV) I think not. As was the custom of the East, sharing bread with an enemy was an act that would make even an enemy become a friend, thus sealing the bond of friendship that cannot be broken. Judas participating in the feet washing and partaking of the Last Supper is more proof that Judas was saved at first. It is not normal to trust your enemy and confide in him. Carry them with you every where you go letting them know your every move. Had Judas been the devil, Jesus would not have permitted him to be this close to Him. Jesus said, "my own familiar friend whom I trusted, which did eat my bread, hath lifted up his heel against me (Psalms 41:9 KJV). This in reference to Judas breaking bread with Jesus at the last supper (John 13:18 KJV).

At one time, the name of Judas was recorded in the book of life (Psalms 69:25-28; Acts 1:20 KJV). In David's 69th Psalm, vs. 28, it is evident he believed a persons name could be blotted out of the book of life. Moses also believed this, as well as God (Exodus 32:32; 32:33) and Jesus (Revelations 3:5: 22:19 KJV).

Judas had a resume second to none. He served as a bishop

(Psalms 109:8; Acts 1:20 KJV), took part in the apostolic ministry (Acts 1:17, 25 KJV), sent forth as one of the twelve to represent Jesus (Matthew 10:4-6 KJV) and received power to cast out unclean spirits and heal all manner of sickness and diseases (Matthew 10:1-8 KJV). Would Jesus give this power to an unsaved person? Certainly not. The scriptures do not say Jesus gave this power to all the disciples except Judas. Jesus says, "and when He had called unto Him, His twelve disciples, He gave them ALL power to do all these things. I might point out again, these twelve men were chosen after Jesus had been praying all night to get the will of God (Matthew 3:13; Luke 6:12-16 KJV). Do you believe Jesus missed the will of God? I think not.

As a preacher, Judas and the disciples were given specific instructions as to what their mission was to be as well as other instructions (Matthew 1: 8-42; 10:7; Mark 3:14 KJV). The holy spirit spoke thru Judas (Matthew 10:19-20 KJV). Does the holy spirit speak thru a sinner or the devil? Further proof that Judas was a part of and fell from, because of sin is recorded in (Acts 1:16-20 KJV).

If Judas was saved, why did Jesus say, "Woe unto him by whom the Son of Man is betrayed?" (Matthew 26:20-24; Mark 14:17-21; Luke 22:21-23). It is true that Judas had eternal life at one time (John 17:2 KJV).

When satan entered into Judas at the supper (Matthew 26:14-16; Luke 22:13:2, 27 KJV), this being the close of the ministry of Jesus (John 13:1 KJV), Judas backslid; fell from grace; lost it all!!!!!!!!!!!! How could the devil enter into himself, or why would he need or have to? This alone would be evidence Judas was not always a devil.

Having backslid, Judas became a thief and a devil (Luke 22:3-6; John 13:2; John 10:1; 12:6; John 6:70 KJV). Greek for devil means adversary or betrayer. Judas was shamed, disgraced and even rejected by the enemy. For anyone to portray Judas as a devil from the beginning and having never been saved, or in grace, is to completely ignore the scriptures.

Even though Judas betrayed Jesus, became a thief and a devil, had he confessed his sin and asked God to forgive him, he could have been saved (Romans 10:10; 1 John 1:9 KJV). All have sinned and to say we have not makes God a liar (1 John 1:10 KJV).

Had Judas repented, not only could he have continued being a great leader, by winning souls and healing multitudes but would have inherited eternal life, a throne over a tribe in Israel and all the glories of the redeemed. Jesus died for all. Everyone who meets the condition, can have eternal life. Whether a person accepts eternal life is a free choice (Mark 16:16; John 3:16; 1 Timothy 2:4; 2 Peter 3:9; Revelations 22:17 KJV).

LIKE SO MANY, DID JUDAS CHOSE DEATH AND HELL?

RECORDED BIBLICAL SUICIDE

Almost daily, we read or learn about someone ending their life. Whether from self-inflicted gun-shot wound, drug overdose, carbon-dioxide poisoning or hanging, it appears that committing suicide has become an acceptable way of dying. The late Dr. Jack Kevorkian made news almost daily with his notoriety of helping terminally ill people intentionally ending their life with a process called euthanasia. Euthanasia is categorized in different ways, which include voluntary, non-voluntary, or involuntary. Voluntary euthanasia is legal in some countries. Non-voluntary euthanasia, where the patient's consent is unavailable, is illegal in all countries. Involuntarily euthanasia, without asking consent or against the patient's will, is also illegal in all countries and is usually considered murder. As of 2006, euthanasia was the most active area of research in contemporary bioethics. In the Netherlands and Belgium, euthanasia is understood as "termination of life by a doctor at the request of a patient". In some countries there is divisive public controversy over the moral, ethical and legal issues of euthanasia. Those who are against euthanasia argue for the sanctity of life, while proponents for euthanasia rights emphasize alleviating suffering, and preserving bodily integrity, self-determination, and personal autonomy. Jurisdictions where euthanasia is legal include the Netherlands, Canada, Columbia, Belgium, Luxembourg, Washington DC, California, Colorado, Oregon, Vermont, Maine, Hawaii, Washington and starting January 1, 2020 New Jersey.

In biblical days, suicide apparently was not a choice way of dying. Of the passages relating to suicide, only two of these figures committed suicide by hanging. The word suicide is not recorded in the Bible. The scriptures refer to taking their life.

Saul

1 Samuel 31: 1-6

When Saul and his soldiers were being over-run by the Philistines, his sons, Jonathan, Abinadad and Melchishua already having been slain, Saul requested his armour-bearer, "Draw your sword, and thrust me, through there-with; lest these uncircumcised come and thrust me through, and abuse me (1 Samuel 31:4 KJV). His armour-bearer would not honor the request of Saul because he was sore afraid. Unable to have someone kill him, Saul took his sword and fell upon it; thus committing suicide. When his armor-bearer saw that Saul was dead, he fell likewise upon his sword, and died with him. In the days of Saul, it was considered by some, an honor to die with their master. Not only did Saul die, but his three sons, his armor-bearer and all his men that had not already escaped (2

Samuel 1:4; 2:8,11 KJV).

Ahithophel, the second recorded suicide, betrayed David and apparently was seeking revenge over David for impregnating Bathshebe, the grand-daughter of Ahithophel (2 Samuel 11:3-5; 2 Samuel 15:31 KJV). Bathshebe was the daughter of Eliam who was the son of Ahithophel, the Gilonite (2 Samuel 23:34 KJV).

Ahithophel, a counselor, had said unto Absalom, "Let me now choose twelve thousand men, and I will arise and pursue after David this night and slay him.(2 Samuel 17:1:2 KJV). The army of Absalom must have been big for this request for twelve thousand soldiers. Upon consulting with another one of his advisors, Absalom rejected the request and stated it is not good at this time (2 Sam. 2:17:7 KJV).

When Ahithophel saw that his counsel was not followed, he saddled his donkey, arose and got him to his city. Having arrived at his house, he put his household in order, hanged himself, and was buried in the sepulchre of his father(2 Samuel 17:23 KJV).

Ahithophel was the Judas of the O.T. in that he not only betrayed David, his best friend, but tried to make a deal with the enemies of David to kill him.

In reference to Ahithophel being the Judas of the O.T., refer to (Psalms 41:9; 55:12-14 KJV).

Judas

Judas was the final biblical character to commit suicide. Having returned the thirty pieces of silver that he had accepted to betray Jesus, he threw them down on the floor of the temple, departed and hanged himself (Matthew 27:3-5 KJV).

EPILOGUE

In today's society, only a gang leader or a crooked politician would surround himself with the type characters that Jesus chose as his disciples. Why He chose these unsavory men to represent Him, without a doubt, each one holds a prominent place in Biblical history. However, the name of Judas is the most recognizable and hated for his betrayal.

Jesus gave Judas unlimited opportunities to have eternal life like he does anyone. Even at the last supper, Judas still could have been true and not betrayed Jesus. Judas refused to listen.

Are you on the verge of becoming a Judas and being eternally lost? Jesus did not forsake Judas; Judas forsook Jesus. Having walked, talked, prayed and broke bread with Jesus, Judas still forsook Him. Jesus has promised, "He would never leave us nor forsake us." (Joshua 1:5; 1 Chronicles 28:20; Hebrews 13:5 KJV)

I trust JESUS THE RENEGADE has been a blessing to you and if you have not accepted Jesus as your savior and soon coming king, don't wait. Now is the accepted time and day of salvation (2 Corinthians 6:2 KJV).

If you are a child of God, don't trade your salvation and eternal life for the things of this world and an eternal hell.

DON'T BE A JUDAS!

ABOUT THE AUTHOR

Larry and Mary are the proud parents of one son, Delane Barton, granddaughter Jessica Barton Akery and two great grandsons, Carter Grant and Chandler William Akery.

Former four term mayor of Talladega, and an accomplished pianist, composer, recording artist, and publisher of eight previous books: *REFLECTION OF AIDS, BOOGER HOLLOW BAD BOY, FROM POLITICS TO PRISON, GANG RAPED, CESS POOL MURDERS, LAST TALLADEGA HANGING, NO DULL MOMENTS WITH LARRY AND MARY, WHEN SIN IS FINISHED.* As a former member of Rotary, Lions, and Toastmaster Int, Larry is an excellent speaker. His wife is an excellent singer.